Elmwood Edition

THE COMPLETE WRITINGS OF JAMES RUSSELL LOWELL

WITH PORTRAITS, ILLUSTRATIONS, AND FACSIMILES

IN SIXTEEN VOLUMES

VOLUME IX

Mr. Lowell in 1875

THE POETICAL WORKS

OF

JAMES RUSSELL LOWELL

IN FIVE VOLUMES

VOLUME I

EARLIER POEMS

THE VISION OF SIR LAUNFAL

BOSTON AND NEW YORK

HOUGHTON, MIFFLIN AND COMPANY

The Riverside Press, Cambridge

1904

PREFATORY NOTE TO THE POEMS

THERE are a great many pieces in these volumes, especially in the first of them, which I would gladly suppress or put into the Coventry of smaller print in an appendix. But " ilka mon maun dree his weird," and the avenging *litera scripta manet* is that of the over-hasty author. Owing to the unjust distinction made by the law between literary and other property, most of what I published prematurely has lost the protection of copyright, and is reprinted by others against my will. I cannot shake off the burthen of my early indiscretions if I would. The best way, perhaps, is to accept with silent contrition the consequences of one's own mistakes, and I have, after much hesitation, consented to the reprinting of the old editions without excision.

I must confess, however, that I have attained this pitch of self-sacrifice only by compulsion, and should have greatly preferred to increase the value of this collection by lessening its bulk. The judicious reader will, I fear, distinguish only too easily what I should wish, in parliamentary phrase, "to be taken as read." As we grow older, we grow the more willing to say, as Petrarca in Landor's "Pentameron" says to Boccaccio, "We neither of us are such poets as we thought ourselves when we were younger."

J. R. L.

9th May, 1890.

CONTENTS

CONTENTS

CONTENTS

MISCELLANEOUS POEMS.

LIST OF ILLUSTRATIONS

EARLIER POEMS

THRENODIA

GONE, gone from us! and shall we see
Those sibyl-leaves of destiny,
Those calm eyes, nevermore?
Those deep, dark eyes so warm and bright,
Wherein the fortunes of the man
Lay slumbering in prophetic light,
In characters a child might scan?
So bright, and gone forth utterly!
Oh stern word — Nevermore!

The stars of those two gentle eyes
Will shine no more on earth;
Quenched are the hopes that had their birth,
As we watched them slowly rise,
Stars of a mother's fate;
And she would read them o'er and o'er,
Pondering, as she sate,
Over their dear astrology,
Which she had conned and conned before,
Deeming she needs must read aright
What was writ so passing bright.
And yet, alas! she knew not why,
Her voice would falter in its song,
And tears would slide from out her eye,
Silent, as they were doing wrong.
Oh stern word — Nevermore!

The tongue that scarce had learned to claim
An entrance to a mother's heart
By that dear talisman, a mother's name,
Sleeps all forgetful of its art!
I loved to see the infant soul
(How mighty in the weakness
Of its untutored meekness!)
Peep timidly from out its nest,
His lips, the while,
Fluttering with half-fledged words,
Or hushing to a smile
That more than words expressed,
When his glad mother on him stole
And snatched him to her breast!
Oh, thoughts were brooding in those eyes,
That would have soared like strong-winged birds
Far, far into the skies,
Gladding the earth with song,
And gushing harmonies,
Had he but tarried with us long!
Oh stern word — Nevermore!

How peacefully they rest,
Crossfolded there
Upon his little breast,
Those small, white hands that ne'er were still before,
But ever sported with his mother's hair,
Or the plain cross that on her breast she wore!
Her heart no more will beat
To feel the touch of that soft palm,
That ever seemed a new surprise
Sending glad thoughts up to her eyes

To bless him with their holy calm, —
Sweet thoughts ! they made her eyes as sweet.
How quiet are the hands
That wove those pleasant bands !
But that they do not rise and sink
With his calm breathing, I should think
That he were dropped asleep.
Alas ! too deep, too deep
Is this his slumber !
Time scarce can number
The years ere he shall wake again.
Oh, may we see his eyelids open then !
Oh stern word — Nevermore !

As the airy gossamere,
Floating in the sunlight clear,
Where'er it toucheth clingeth tightly,
Round glossy leaf or stump unsightly,
So from his spirit wandered out
Tendrils spreading all about,
Knitting all things to its thrall
With a perfect love of all :
Oh stern word — Nevermore !

He did but float a little way
Adown the stream of time,
With dreamy eyes watching the ripples play,
Or hearkening their fairy chime ;
His slender sail
Ne'er felt the gale ;
He did but float a little way,
And, putting to the shore

While yet 't was early day,
Went calmly on his way,
To dwell with us no more !
No jarring did he feel,
No grating on his shallop's keel ;
A strip of silver sand
Mingled the waters with the land
Where he was seen no more :
Oh stern word — Nevermore !

Full short his journey was ; no dust
Of earth unto his sandals clave ;
The weary weight that old men must,
He bore not to the grave.
He seemed a cherub who had lost his way
And wandered hither, so his stay
With us was short, and 't was most meet
That he should be no delver in earth's clod,
Nor need to pause and cleanse his feet
To stand before his God :
Oh blest word — Evermore !

THE SIRENS

THE sea is lonely, the sea is dreary,
The sea is restless and uneasy ;
Thou seekest quiet, thou art weary,
Wandering thou knowest not whither ; —
Our little isle is green and breezy,
Come and rest thee ! Oh come hither,

Come to this peaceful home of ours,
    Where evermore
The low west-wind creeps panting up the shore
To be at rest among the flowers;
Full of rest, the green moss lifts,
   As the dark waves of the sea
Draw in and out of rocky rifts,
   Calling solemnly to thee
With voices deep and hollow, —
   " To the shore
   Follow! Oh, follow!
   To be at rest forevermore!
     Forevermore!"

Look how the gray old Ocean
From the depth of his heart rejoices,
Heaving with a gentle motion,
When he hears our restful voices;
List how he sings in an undertone,
Chiming with our melody;
And all sweet sounds of earth and air
Melt into one low voice alone,
That murmurs over the weary sea,
And seems to sing from everywhere, —
" Here mayst thou harbor peacefully,
Here mayst thou rest from the aching oar;
   Turn thy curvëd prow ashore,
And in our green isle rest forevermore!
     Forevermore!"
And Echo half wakes in the wooded hill,
   And, to her heart so calm and deep,
   Murmurs over in her sleep,

Doubtfully pausing and murmuring still,
   " Evermore ! "
     Thus, on Life's weary sea,
     Heareth the marinere
     Voices sweet, from far and near,
     Ever singing low and clear,
     Ever singing longingly.

   Is it not better here to be,
Than to be toiling late and soon ?
In the dreary night to see
Nothing but the blood-red moon
Go up and down into the sea ;
Or, in the loneliness of day,
   To see the still seals only
Solemnly lift their faces gray,
   Making it yet more lonely ?
Is it not better than to hear
Only the sliding of the wave
Beneath the plank, and feel so near
A cold and lonely grave,
A restless grave, where thou shalt lie
Even in death unquietly ?
Look down beneath thy wave-worn bark,
   Lean over the side and see
The leaden eye of the sidelong shark
     Upturnëd patiently,
   Ever waiting there for thee :
Look down and see those shapeless forms,
   Which ever keep their dreamless sleep
   Far down within the gloomy deep,
And only stir themselves in storms,

Rising like islands from beneath,
And snorting through the angry spray,
As the frail vessel perisheth
In the whirls of their unwieldy play;
   Look down! Look down!
Upon the seaweed, slimy and dark,
That waves its arms so lank and brown,
  Beckoning for thee!
Look down beneath thy wave-worn bark
  Into the cold depth of the sea!
   Look down! Look down!
  Thus, on Life's lonely sea,
  Heareth the marinere
  Voices sad, from far and near,
  Ever singing full of fear,
  Ever singing drearfully.

 Here all is pleasant as a dream;
The wind scarce shaketh down the dew,
The green grass floweth like a stream
  Into the ocean's blue;
   Listen! Oh, listen!
Here is a gush of many streams,
 A song of many birds,
And every wish and longing seems
Lulled to a numbered flow of words, —
   Listen! Oh, listen!
Here ever hum the golden bees
Underneath full-blossomed trees,
At once with glowing fruit and flowers crowned; —
So smooth the sand, the yellow sand,
That thy keel will not grate as it touches the land;

All around with a slumberous sound,
The singing waves slide up the strand,
And there, where the smooth, wet pebbles be,
The waters gurgle longingly,
As if they fain would seek the shore,
To be at rest from the ceaseless roar,
To be at rest forevermore, —
    Forevermore.
  Thus, on Life's gloomy sea,
  Heareth the marinere
  Voices sweet, from far and near,
  Ever singing in his ear,
" Here is rest and peace for thee ! "

IRENÉ

Hers is a spirit deep, and crystal-clear ;
Calmly beneath her earnest face it lies,
Free without boldness, meek without a fear,
Quicker to look than speak its sympathies ;
Far down into her large and patient eyes
I gaze, deep-drinking of the infinite,
As, in the mid-watch of a clear, still night,
I look into the fathomless blue skies.

So circled lives she with Love's holy light,
That from the shade of self she walketh free ;
The garden of her soul still keepeth she
An Eden where the snake did never enter ;
She hath a natural, wise sincerity,

A simple truthfulness, and these have lent her
A dignity as moveless as the centre;
So that no influence of our earth can stir
Her steadfast courage, nor can take away
The holy peacefulness, which night and day,
Unto her queenly soul doth minister.

Most gentle is she; her large charity
(An all unwitting, childlike gift in her)
Not freer is to give than meek to bear;
And, though herself not unacquaint with care,
Hath in her heart wide room for all that be, —
Her heart that hath no secrets of its own,
But open is as eglantine full blown.
Cloudless forever is her brow serene,
Speaking calm hope and trust within her, whence
Welleth a noiseless spring of patience,
That keepeth all her life so fresh, so green
And full of holiness, that every look,
The greatness of her woman's soul revealing,
Unto me bringeth blessing, and a feeling
As when I read in God's own holy book.

A graciousness in giving that doth make
The small'st gift greatest, and a sense most meek
Of worthiness, that doth not fear to take
From others, but which always fears to speak
Its thanks in utterance, for the giver's sake; —
The deep religion of a thankful heart,
Which rests instinctively in Heaven's clear law
With a full peace, that never can depart
From its own steadfastness; — a holy awe

For holy things, — not those which men call holy,
But such as are revealëd to the eyes
Of a true woman's soul bent down and lowly
Before the face of daily mysteries ; —
A love that blossoms soòn, but ripens slowly
To the full goldenness of fruitful prime,
Enduring with a firmness that defies
All shallow tricks of circumstance and time,
By a sure insight knowing where to cling,
And where it clingeth never withering ; —
These are Irené's dowry, which no fate
Can shake from their serene, deep-builded state.

    In-seeing sympathy is hers, which chasteneth
No less than loveth, scorning to be bound
With fear of blame, and yet which ever hasteneth
To pour the balm of kind looks on the wound,
If they be wounds which such sweet teaching makes,
Giving itself a pang for others' sakes ;
No want of faith, that chills with sidelong eye,
Hath she ; no jealousy, no Levite pride
That passeth by upon the other side ;
For in her soul there never dwelt a lie.
Right from the hand of God her spirit came
Unstained, and she hath ne'er forgotten whence
It came, nor wandered far from thence,
But laboreth to keep her still the same,
Near to her place of birth, that she may not
Soil her white raiment with an earthly spot.

    Yet sets she not her soul so steadily
Above, that she forgets her ties to earth,

But her whole thought would almost seem to be
How to make glad one lowly human hearth;
For with a gentle courage she doth strive
In thought and word and feeling so to live
As to make earth next heaven; and her heart
Herein doth show its most exceeding worth,
That, bearing in our frailty her just part,
She hath not shrunk from evils of this life,
But hath gone calmly forth into the strife,
And all its sins and sorrows hath withstood
With lofty strength of patient womanhood:
For this I love her great soul more than all,
That, being bound, like us, with earthly thrall,
She walks so bright and heaven-like therein, —
Too wise, too meek, too womanly, to sin.

Like a lone star through riven storm-clouds seen
By sailors, tempest-tost upon the sea,
Telling of rest and peaceful heavens nigh,
Unto my soul her star-like soul hath been,
Her sight as full of hope and calm to me; —
For she unto herself hath builded high
A home serene, wherein to lay her head,
Earth's noblest thing, a Woman perfected.

SERENADE

FROM the close-shut windows gleams no spark,
The night is chilly, the night is dark,
The poplars shiver, the pine-trees moan,
My hair by the autumn breeze is blown,
Under thy window I sing alone,
Alone, alone, ah woe! alone!

The darkness is pressing coldly around,
The windows shake with a lonely sound,
The stars are hid and the night is drear,
The heart of silence throbs in thine ear,
In thy chamber thou sittest alone,
Alone, alone, ah woe! alone!

The world is happy, the world is wide,
Kind hearts are beating on every side;
Ah, why should we lie so coldly curled
Alone in the shell of this great world?
Why should we any more be alone?
Alone, alone, ah woe! alone!

Oh, 't is a bitter and dreary word,
The saddest by man's ear ever heard!
We each are young, we each have a heart,
Why stand we ever coldly apart?
Must we forever, then, be alone?
Alone, alone, ah woe! alone!

WITH A PRESSED FLOWER

THIS little blossom from afar
Hath come from other lands to thine ;
For, once, its white and drooping star
Could see its shadow in the Rhine.

Perchance some fair-haired German maid
Hath plucked one from the selfsame stalk,
And numbered over, half afraid,
Its petals in her evening walk.

" He loves me, loves me not," she cries ;
" He loves me more than earth or heaven ! "
And then glad tears have filled her eyes
To find the number was uneven.

And thou must count its petals well,
Because it is a gift from me ;
And the last one of all shall tell
Something I 've often told to thee.

But here at home, where we were born,
Thou wilt find blossoms just as true,
Down-bending every summer morn,
With freshness of New England dew.

For Nature, ever kind to love,
Hath granted them the same sweet tongue,
Whether with German skies above,
Or here our granite rocks among.

THE BEGGAR

A BEGGAR through the world am I,
From place to place I wander by.
Fill up my pilgrim's scrip for me,
For Christ's sweet sake and charity !

A little of thy steadfastness,
Rounded with leafy gracefulness,
Old oak, give me,
That the world's blasts may round me blow,
And I yield gently to and fro,
While my stout-hearted trunk below
And firm-set roots unshaken be.

Some of thy stern, unyielding might,
Enduring still through day and night
Rude tempest-shock and withering blight,
That I may keep at bay
The changeful April sky of chance
And the strong tide of circumstance, —
Give me, old granite gray.

Some of thy pensiveness serene,
Some of thy never-dying green,
Put in this scrip of mine,
That griefs may fall like snow-flakes light,
And deck me in a robe of white,
Ready to be an angel bright,
O sweetly mournful pine.

A little of thy merriment,
Of thy sparkling, light content,
Give me, my cheerful brook,
That I may still be full of glee
And gladsomeness, where'er I be,
Though fickle fate hath prisoned me
In some neglected nook.

Ye have been very kind and good
To me, since I 've been in the wood ;
Ye have gone nigh to fill my heart ;
But good-bye, kind friends, every one,
I 've far to go ere set of sun ;
Of all good things I would have part,
The day was high ere I could start,
And so my journey 's scarce begun.

Heaven help me ! how could I forget
To beg of thee, dear violet !
Some of thy modesty,
That blossoms here as well, unseen,
As if before the world thou 'dst been,
Oh, give, to strengthen me.

I

MY LOVE

I

NOT as all other women are
Is she that to my soul is dear;
Her glorious fancies come from far,
Beneath the silver evening-star,
And yet her heart is ever near.

II

Great feelings hath she of her own,
Which lesser souls may never know;
God giveth them to her alone,
And sweet they are as any tone
Wherewith the wind may choose to blow.

III

Yet in herself she dwelleth not,
Although no home were half so fair;
No simplest duty is forgot,
Life hath no dim and lowly spot
That doth not in her sunshine share.

IV

She doeth little kindnesses,
Which most leave undone, or despise:
For naught that sets one heart at ease,
And giveth happiness or peace,
Is low-esteemèd in her eyes.

V

She hath no scorn of common things,
And, though she seem of other birth,
Round us her heart intwines and clings,
And patiently she folds her wings
To tread the humble paths of earth.

VI

Blessing she is : God made her so,
And deeds of week-day holiness
Fall from her noiseless as the snow,
Nor hath she ever chanced to know
That aught were easier than to bless.

VII

She is most fair, and thereunto
Her life doth rightly harmonize ;
Feeling or thought that was not true
Ne'er made less beautiful the blue
Unclouded heaven of her eyes.

VIII

She is a woman : one in whom
The spring-time of her childish years
Hath never lost its fresh perfume,
Though knowing well that life hath room
For many blights and many tears.

IX

I love her with a love as still
As a broad river's peaceful might,

Which, by high tower and lowly mill,
Seems following its own wayward will,
And yet doth ever flow aright.

x

And, on its full, deep breast serene,
Like quiet isles my duties lie;
It flows around them and between,
And makes them fresh and fair and green,
Sweet homes wherein to live and die.

SUMMER STORM

UNTREMULOUS in the river clear,
Toward the sky's image, hangs the imaged bridge;
    So still the air that I can hear
The slender clarion of the unseen midge;
    Out of the stillness, with a gathering creep,
Like rising wind in leaves, which now decreases,
Now lulls, now swells, and all the while increases,
    The huddling trample of a drove of sheep
Tilts the loose planks, and then as gradually ceases
    In dust on the other side; life's emblem deep,
A confused noise between two silences,
Finding at last in dust precarious peace.
On the wide marsh the purple-blossomed grasses
    Soak up the sunshine; sleeps the brimming tide,
Save when the wedge-shaped wake in silence passes
    Of some slow water-rat, whose sinuous glide
Wavers the sedge's emerald shade from side to side;

But up the west, like a rock-shivered surge,
  Climbs a great cloud edged with sun-whitened spray;
Huge whirls of foam boil toppling o'er its verge,
  And falling still it seems, and yet it climbs alway.

      Suddenly all the sky is hid
      As with the shutting of a lid,
  One by one great drops are falling
        Doubtful and slow,
    Down the pane they are crookedly crawling,
        And the wind breathes low;
  Slowly the circles widen on the river,
      Widen and mingle, one and all;
  Here and there the slenderer flowers shiver,
      Struck by an icy rain-drop's fall.

Now on the hills I hear the thunder mutter,
    The wind is gathering in the west;
The upturned leaves first whiten and flutter,
    Then droop to a fitful rest;
Up from the stream with sluggish flap
  Struggles the gull and floats away;
Nearer and nearer rolls the thunder-clap, —
  We shall not see the sun go down to-day:
Now leaps the wind on the sleepy marsh,
  And tramples the grass with terrified feet,
The startled river turns leaden and harsh.
  You can hear the quick heart of the tempest beat.

    Look! look! that livid flash!
And instantly follows the rattling thunder,
As if some cloud-crag, split asunder,
      Fell, splintering with a ruinous crash,

On the Earth, which crouches in silence under;
   And now a solid gray wall of rain
Shuts off the landscape, mile by mile;
   For a breath's space I see the blue wood again,
And ere the next heart-beat, the wind-hurled pile,
   That seemed but now a league aloof,
   Bursts crackling o'er the sun-parched roof;
Against the windows the storm comes dashing,
Through tattered foliage the hail tears crashing,
        The blue lightning flashes,
        The rapid hail clashes,
      The white waves are tumbling,
        And, in one baffled roar,
     Like the toothless sea mumbling
       A rock-bristled shore,
      The thunder is rumbling
      And crashing and crumbling, —
   Will silence return nevermore?

      Hush! Still as death,
      The tempest holds his breath
    As from a sudden will;
The rain stops short, but from the eaves
You see it drop, and hear it from the leaves,
    All is so bodingly still;
      Again, now, now, again
Plashes the rain in heavy gouts,
     The crinkled lightning
     Seems ever brightening,
      And loud and long
   Again the thunder shouts
      His battle-song, —

One quivering flash,
One wildering crash,
Followed by silence dead and dull,
As if the cloud, let go,
Leapt bodily below
To whelm the earth in one mad overthrow,
And then a total lull.

Gone, gone, so soon!
No more my half-dazed fancy there,
Can shape a giant in the air,
No more I see his streaming hair,
The writhing portent of his form; —
The pale and quiet moon
Makes her calm forehead bare,
And the last fragments of the storm,
Like shattered rigging from a fight at sea,
Silent and few, are drifting over me.

LOVE

TRUE Love is but a humble, low-born thing,
And hath its food served up in earthen ware;
It is a thing to walk with, hand in hand,
Through the every-dayness of this work-day world,
Baring its tender feet to every flint,
Yet letting not one heart-beat go astray
From Beauty's law of plainness and content;
A simple, fireside thing, whose quiet smile
Can warm earth's poorest hovel to a home;

Which, when our autumn cometh, as it must,
And life in the chill wind shivers bare and leafless,
Shall still be blest with Indian-summer youth
In bleak November, and, with thankful heart,
Smile on its ample stores of garnered fruit,
As full of sunshine to our aged eyes
As when it nursed the blossoms of our spring.
Such is true Love, which steals into the heart
With feet as silent as the lightsome dawn
That kisses smooth the rough brows of the dark,
And hath its will through blissful gentleness,
Not like a rocket, which, with passionate glare,
Whirs suddenly up, then bursts, and leaves the night
Painfully quivering on the dazëd eyes ;
A love that gives and takes, that seeth faults,
Not with flaw-seeking eyes like needle points,
But loving-kindly ever looks them down
With the o'ercoming faith that still forgives ;
A love that shall be new and fresh each hour,
As is the sunset's golden mystery,
Or the sweet coming of the evening-star,
Alike, and yet most unlike, every day,
And seeming ever best and fairest *now* ;
A love that doth not kneel for what it seeks,
But faces Truth and Beauty as their peer,
Showing its worthiness of noble thoughts
By a clear sense of inward nobleness ;
A love that in its object findeth not
All grace and beauty, and enough to sate
Its thirst of blessing, but, in all of good
Found there, sees but the Heaven-implanted types
Of good and beauty in the soul of man,

And traces, in the simplest heart that beats,
A family-likeness to its chosen one,
That claims of it the rights of brotherhood.
For love is blind but with the fleshly eye,
That so its inner sight may be more clear;
And outward shows of beauty only so
Are needful at the first, as is a hand
To guide and to uphold an infant's steps:
Fine natures need them not: their earnest look
Pierces the body's mask of thin disguise,
And beauty ever is to them revealed,
Behind the unshapeliest, meanest lump of clay,
With arms outstretched and eager face ablaze,
Yearning to be but understood and loved.

TO PERDITA, SINGING

THY voice is like a fountain,
   Leaping up in clear moonshine;
Silver, silver, ever mounting,
          Ever sinking,
          Without thinking,
   To that brimful heart of thine.
Every sad and happy feeling,
Thou hast had in bygone years,
Through thy lips comes stealing, stealing,
          Clear and low;
All thy smiles and all thy tears
   In thy voice awaken,
   And sweetness, wove of joy and woe,
      From their teaching it hath taken:

Feeling and music move together,
Like a swan and shadow ever
Floating on a sky-blue river
In a day of cloudless weather.

It hath caught a touch of sadness,
    Yet it is not sad;
It hath tones of clearest gladness,
    Yet it is not glad;
A dim, sweet twilight voice it is
  Where to-day's accustomed blue
Is over-grayed with memories,
  With starry feelings quivered through.

Thy voice is like a fountain
Leaping up in sunshine bright,
  And I never weary counting
Its clear droppings, lone and single,
Or when in one full gush they mingle,
  Shooting in melodious light.

Thine is music such as yields
Feelings of old brooks and fields,
And, around this pent-up room,
Sheds a woodland, free perfume;
  Oh, thus forever sing to me!
    Oh, thus forever!
The green, bright grass of childhood bring to
    me,
  Flowing like an emerald river,
  And the bright blue skies above!
Oh, sing them back, as fresh as ever,

Into the bosom of my love, —
The sunshine and the merriment,
The unsought, evergreen content,
   Of that never cold time,
The joy, that, like a clear breeze, went
   Through and through the old time!

Peace sits within thine eyes,
   With white hands crossed in joyful rest,
While, through thy lips and face, arise
The melodies from out thy breast;
     She sits and sings,
     With folded wings
     And white arms crost,
" Weep not for bygone things,
     They are not lost:
The beauty which the summer time
O'er thine opening spirit shed,
The forest oracles sublime
That filled thy soul with joyous dread,
The scent of every smallest flower
That made thy heart sweet for an hour,
Yea, every holy influence,
Flowing to thee, thou knewest not whence,
In thine eyes to-day is seen,
Fresh as it hath ever been;
Promptings of Nature, beckonings sweet,
Whatever led thy childish feet,
Still will linger unawares
The guiders of thy silver hairs;
Every look and every word
Which thou givest forth to-day,

Tell of the singing of the bird
Whose music stilled thy boyish play."

Thy voice is like a fountain,
Twinkling up in sharp starlight,
When the moon behind the mountain
Dims the low East with faintest white,
      Ever darkling,
      Ever sparkling,
  We know not if 't is dark or bright;
But, when the great moon hath rolled round,
  And, sudden-slow, its solemn power
Grows from behind its black, clear-edgëd bound,
  No spot of dark the fountain keepeth,
  But, swift as opening eyelids, leapeth
  Into a waving silver flower.

THE MOON

  My soul was like the sea,
  Before the moon was made,
Moaning in vague immensity,
  Of its own strength afraid,
  Unrestful and unstaid.
Through every rift it foamed in vain,
  About its earthly prison,
Seeking some unknown thing in pain,
And sinking restless back again,
  For yet no moon had risen:

Its only voice a vast dumb moan,
    Of utterless anguish speaking,
It lay unhopefully alone,
    And lived but in an aimless seeking.

So was my soul; but when 't was full
    Of unrest to o'erloading,
A voice of something beautiful
    Whispered a dim foreboding,
And yet so soft, so sweet, so low,
It had not more of joy than woe;

And, as the sea doth oft lie still,
    Making its waters meet,
As if by an unconscious will,
    For the moon's silver feet,
So lay my soul within mine eyes
When thou, its guardian moon, didst rise.

And now, howe'er its waves above
    May toss and seem uneaseful,
One strong, eternal law of Love,
    With guidance sure and peaceful,
As calm and natural as breath,
Moves its great deeps through life and death.

REMEMBERED MUSIC

A FRAGMENT

THICK-RUSHING, like an ocean vast
   Of bisons the far prairie shaking,
The notes crowd heavily and fast
As surfs, one plunging while the last
   Draws seaward from its foamy breaking.

Or in low murmurs they began,
   Rising and rising momently,
As o'er a harp Æolian
A fitful breeze, until they ran
   Up to a sudden ecstasy.

And then, like minute-drops of rain
   Ringing in water silverly,
They lingering dropped and dropped again,
Till it was almost like a pain
   To listen when the next would be.

SONG

TO M. L.

A LILY thou wast when I saw thee first,
   A lily-bud not opened quite,
   That hourly grew more pure and white,
By morning, and noontide, and evening nursed:

In all of Nature thou hadst thy share ;
    Thou wast waited on
    By the wind and sun ;
The rain and the dew for thee took care ;
It seemed thou never couldst be more fair.

A lily thou wast when I saw thee first,
    A lily-bud ; but oh, how strange,
    How full of wonder was the change,
When, ripe with all sweetness, thy full bloom burst !
How did the tears to my glad eyes start,
    When the woman-flower
    Reached its blossoming hour,
And I saw the warm deeps of thy golden heart !

Glad death may pluck thee, but never before
    The gold dust of thy bloom divine
    Hath dropped from thy heart into mine,
To quicken its faint germs of heavenly lore ;
  For no breeze comes nigh thee but carries away
    Some impulses bright
    Of fragrance and light,
Which fall upon souls that are lone and astray,
To plant fruitful hopes of the flower of day.

ALLEGRA

I would more natures were like thine,
  That never casts a glance before,
Thou Hebe, who thy heart's bright wine
  So lavishly to all dost pour,
That we who drink forget to pine,
  And can but dream of bliss in store.

Thou canst not see a shade in life;
  With sunward instinct thou dost rise,
And, leaving clouds below at strife,
  Gazest undazzled at the skies,
With all their blazing splendors rife,
  A songful lark with eagle's eyes.

Thou wast some foundling whom the Hours
  Nursed, laughing, with the milk of Mirth;
Some influence more gay than ours
  Hath ruled thy nature from its birth,
As if thy natal stars were flowers
  That shook their seeds round thee on earth.

And thou, to lull thine infant rest,
  Wast cradled like an Indian child;
All pleasant winds from south and west
  With lullabies thine ears beguiled,
Rocking thee in thine oriole's nest,
  Till Nature looked at thee and smiled.

Thine every fancy seems to borrow
  A sunlight from thy childish years,
Making a golden cloud of sorrow,
  A hope-lit rainbow out of tears, —
Thy heart is certain of to-morrow,
  Though 'yond to-day it never peers.

I would more natures were like thine,
  So innocently wild and free,
Whose sad thoughts, even, leap and shine,
  Like sunny wavelets in the sea,
Making us mindless of the brine,
  In gazing on the brilliancy.

THE FOUNTAIN

Into the sunshine,
  Full of the light,
Leaping and flashing
  From morn till night;

Into the moonlight,
  Whiter than snow,
Waving so flower-like
  When the winds blow;

Into the starlight
  Rushing in spray,
Happy at midnight,
  Happy by day;

1

Ever in motion,
   Blithesome and cheery,
Still climbing heavenward,
   Never aweary;

Glad of all weathers,
   Still seeming best,
Upward or downward,
   Motion thy rest;

Full of a nature
   Nothing can tame,
Changed every moment,
   Ever the same;

Ceaseless aspiring,
   Ceaseless content,
Darkness or sunshine
   Thy element;

Glorious fountain,
   Let my heart be
Fresh, changeful, constant,
   Upward, like thee!

ODE

I

In the old days of awe and keen-eyed wonder,
  The Poet's song with blood-warm truth was rife;
He saw the mysteries which circle under
  The outward shell and skin of daily life.
Nothing to him were fleeting time and fashion,
  His soul was led by the eternal law;
There was in him no hope of fame, no passion,
  But with calm, godlike eyes he only saw.
He did not sigh o'er heroes dead and buried,
  Chief-mourner at the Golden Age's hearse,
Nor deem that souls whom Charon grim had ferried
  Alone were fitting themes of epic verse:
He could believe the promise of to-morrow,
  And feel the wondrous meaning of to-day;
He had a deeper faith in holy sorrow
  Than the world's seeming loss could take away.
To know the heart of all things was his duty,
  All things did sing to him to make him wise,
And, with a sorrowful and conquering beauty,
  The soul of all looked grandly from his eyes.
He gazed on all within him and without him,
  He watched the flowing of Time's steady tide,
And shapes of glory floated all about him
  And whispered to him, and he prophesied.
Than all men he more fearless was and freer,
  And all his brethren cried with one accord, —

" Behold the holy man ! Behold the Seer !
   Him who hath spoken with the unseen Lord ! "
He to his heart with large embrace had taken
   The universal sorrow of mankind,
And, from that root, a shelter never shaken,
   The tree of wisdom grew with sturdy rind.
He could interpret well the wondrous voices
   Which to the calm and silent spirit come ;
He knew that the One Soul no more rejoices
   In the star's anthem than the insect's hum.
He in his heart was ever meek and humble,
   And yet with kingly pomp his numbers ran,
As he foresaw how all things false should crumble
   Before the free, uplifted soul of man :
And, when he was made full to overflowing
   With all the loveliness of heaven and earth,
Out rushed his song, like molten iron glowing,
   To show God sitting by the humblest hearth.
With calmest courage he was ever ready
   To teach that action was the truth of thought,
And, with strong arm and purpose firm and steady,
   An anchor for the drifting world he wrought.
So did he make the meanest man partaker
   Of all his brother-gods unto him gave ;
All souls did reverence him and name him Maker,
   And when he died heaped temples on his grave.
And still his deathless words of light are swimming
   Serene throughout the great deep infinite
Of human soul, unwaning and undimming,
   To cheer and guide the mariner at night.

II

But now the Poet is an empty rhymer
   Who lies with idle elbow on the grass,
And fits his singing, like a cunning timer,
   To all men's prides and fancies as they pass.
Not his the song, which, in its metre holy,
   Chimes with the music of the eternal stars,
Humbling the tyrant, lifting up the lowly,
   And sending sun through the soul's prison-bars.
Maker no more, — oh no! unmaker rather,
   For he unmakes who doth not all put forth
The power given freely by our loving Father
   To show the body's dross, the spirit's worth.
Awake! great spirit of the ages olden!
   Shiver the mists that hide thy starry lyre,
And let man's soul be yet again beholden
   To thee for wings to soar to her desire.
Oh, prophesy no more to-morrow's splendor,
   Be no more shamefaced to speak out for Truth,
Lay on her altar all the gushings tender,
   The hope, the fire, the loving faith of youth!
Oh, prophesy no more the Maker's coming,
   Say not his onward footsteps thou canst hear
In the dim void, like to the awful humming
   Of the great wings of some new-lighted sphere!
Oh, prophesy no more, but be the Poet!
   This longing was but granted unto thee
That, when all beauty thou couldst feel and know it,
   That beauty in its highest thou shouldst be.
O thou who moanest tost with sealike longings,
   Who dimly hearest voices call on thee,

Whose soul is overfilled with mighty throngings
   Of love, and fear, and glorious agony,
Thou of the toil-strung hands and iron sinews
   And soul by Mother Earth with freedom fed,
In whom the hero-spirit yet continues,
   The old free nature is not chained or dead,
Arouse! let thy soul break in music-thunder,
   Let loose the ocean that is in thee pent,
Pour forth thy hope, thy fear, thy love, thy wonder,
   And tell the age what all its signs have meant.
Where'er thy wildered crowd of brethren jostles,
   Where'er there lingers but a shadow of wrong,
There still is need of martyrs and apostles,
   There still are texts for never-dying song:
From age to age man's still aspiring spirit
   Finds wider scope and sees with clearer eyes,
And thou in larger measure dost inherit
   What made thy great forerunners free and wise.
Sit thou enthronëd where the Poet's mountain
   Above the thunder lifts its silent peak,
And roll thy songs down like a gathering fountain,
   They all may drink and find the rest they seek.
Sing! there shall silence grow in earth and heaven,
   A silence of deep awe and wondering;
For, listening gladly, bend the angels, even,
   To hear a mortal like an angel sing.

III

Among the toil-worn poor my soul is seeking
   For who shall bring the Maker's name to light,
To be the voice of that almighty speaking
   Which every age demands to do it right.

Proprieties our silken bards environ;
   He who would be the tongue of this wide land
Must string his harp with chords of sturdy iron
   And strike it with a toil-imbrownëd hand;
One who hath dwelt with Nature well attended,
   Who hath learnt wisdom from her mystic books,
Whose soul with all her countless lives hath blended,
   So that all beauty awes us in his looks;
Who not with body's waste his soul hath pampered,
   Who as the clear northwestern wind is free,
Who walks with Form's observances unhampered,
   And follows the One Will obediently;
Whose eyes, like windows on a breezy summit,
   Control a lovely prospect every way;
Who doth not sound God's sea with earthly plummet,
   And find a bottom still of worthless clay;
Who heeds not how the lower gusts are working,
   Knowing that one sure wind blows on above,
And sees, beneath the foulest faces lurking,
   One God-built shrine of reverence and love;
Who sees all stars that wheel their shining marches
   Around the centre fixed of Destiny,
Where the encircling soul serene o'erarches
   The moving globe of being like a sky;
Who feels that God and Heaven's great deeps are nearer
   Him to whose heart his fellow man is nigh,
Who doth not hold his soul's own freedom dearer
   Than that of all his brethren, low or high;
Who to the Right can feel himself the truer
   For being gently patient with the wrong,
Who sees a brother in the evil-doer,
   And finds in Love the heart's-blood of his song; —

This, this is he for whom the world is waiting
   To sing the beatings of its mighty heart,
Too long hath it been patient with the grating
   Of scrannel-pipes, and heard it misnamed Art.
To him the smiling soul of man shall listen,
   Laying awhile its crown of thorns aside,
And once again in every eye shall glisten
   The glory of a nature satisfied.
His verse shall have a great commanding motion,
   Heaving and swelling with a melody
Learnt of the sky, the river, and the ocean,
   And all the pure, majestic things that be.
Awake, then, thou! we pine for thy great presence
   To make us feel the soul once more sublime,
We are of far too infinite an essence
   To rest contented with the lies of Time.
Speak out! and lo! a hush of deepest wonder
   Shall sink o'er all this many-voicëd scene,
As when a sudden burst of rattling thunder
   Shatters the blueness of a sky serene.

THE FATHERLAND

Where is the true man's fatherland?
   Is it where he by chance is born?
   Doth not the yearning spirit scorn
In such scant borders to be spanned?
Oh yes! his fatherland must be
As the blue heaven wide and free!

Is it alone where freedom is,
  Where God is God and man is man ? .
  Doth he not claim a broader span
For the soul's love of home than this ?
Oh yes ! his fatherland must be
As the blue heaven wide and free !

Where'er a human heart doth wear
  Joy's myrtle-wreath or sorrow's gyves,
  Where'er a human spirit strives
After a life more true and fair,
There is the true man's birthplace grand,
His is a world-wide fatherland !

Where'er a single slave doth pine,
  Where'er one man may help another, —
  Thank God for such a birthright, brother, —
That spot of earth is thine and mine !
There is the true man's birthplace grand,
His is a world-wide fatherland !

TIIE FORLORN

THE night is dark, the stinging sleet,
  Swept by the bitter gusts of air,
Drives whistling down the lonely street,
  And glazes on the pavement bare.

The street-lamps flare and struggle dim
  Through the gray sleet-clouds as they pass,

Or, governed by a boisterous whim,
    Drop down and rustle on the glass.

One poor, heart-broken, outcast girl
    Faces the east-wind's searching flaws,
And, as about her heart they whirl,
    Her tattered cloak more tightly draws.

The flat brick walls look cold and bleak,
    Her bare feet to the sidewalk freeze;
Yet dares she not a shelter seek,
    Though faint with hunger and disease.

The sharp storm cuts her forehead bare,
    And, piercing through her garments thin,
Beats on her shrunken breast, and there
    Makes colder the cold heart within.

She lingers where a ruddy glow
    Streams outward through an open shutter,
Adding more bitterness to woe,
    More loneness to desertion utter.

One half the cold she had not felt
    Until she saw this gush of light
Spread warmly forth, and seem to melt
    Its slow way through the deadening night.

She hears a woman's voice within,
    Singing sweet words her childhood knew,
And years of misery and sin
    Furl off, and leave her heaven blue.

Her freezing heart, like one who sinks
  Outwearied in the drifting snow,
Drowses to deadly sleep and thinks
  No longer of its hopeless woe :

Old fields, and clear blue summer days,
  Old meadows, green with grass, and trees
That shimmer through the trembling haze
  And whiten in the western breeze,

Old faces, all the friendly past
  Rises within her heart again,
And sunshine from her childhood cast
  Makes summer of the icy rain.

Enhaloed by a mild, warm glow,
  From man's humanity apart,
She hears old footsteps wandering slow
  Through the lone chambers of the heart.

Outside the porch before the door,
  Her cheek upon the cold, hard stone,
She lies, no longer foul and poor,
  No longer dreary and alone.

Next morning something heavily
  Against the opening door did weigh,
And there, from sin and sorrow free,
  A woman on the threshold lay.

A smile upon the wan lips told
  That she had found a calm release,

And that, from out the want and cold,
   The song had borne her soul in peace.

For, whom the heart of man shuts out,
   Sometimes the heart of God takes in,
And fences them all round about
   With silence mid the world's loud din ;

And one of his great charities
   Is Music, and it doth not scorn
To close the lids upon the eyes
   Of the polluted and forlorn ;

Far was she from her childhood's home,
   Farther in guilt had wandered thence,
Yet thither it had bid her come
   To die in maiden innocence.

MIDNIGHT

THE moon shines white and silent
   On the mist, which, like a tide
Of some enchanted ocean,
   O'er the wide marsh doth glide,
Spreading its ghost-like billows
   Silently far and wide.

A vague and starry magic
   Makes all things mysteries,

And lures the earth's dumb spirit
  Up to the longing skies ;
I seem to hear dim whispers,
  And tremulous replies.

The fireflies o'er the meadow
  In pulses come and go ;
The elm-trees' heavy shadow
  Weighs on the grass below ;
And faintly from the distance
  The dreaming cock doth crow.

All things look strange and mystic,
  The very bushes swell
And take wild shapes and motions,
  As if beneath a spell ;
They seem not the same lilacs
  From childhood known so well.

The snow of deepest silence
  O'er everything doth fall,
So beautiful and quiet,
  And yet so like a pall ;
As if all life were ended,
  And rest were come to all.

O wild and wondrous midnight,
  There is a might in thee
To make the charmëd body
  Almost like spirit be,
And give it some faint glimpses
  Of immortality !

A PRAYER

God! do not let my loved one die,
  But rather wait until the time
That I am grown in purity
  Enough to enter thy pure clime,
Then take me, I will gladly go,
So that my love remain below!

Oh, let her stay! She is by birth
  What I through death must learn to be;
We need her more on our poor earth
  Than thou canst need in heaven with thee:
She hath her wings already, I
Must burst this earth-shell ere I fly.

Then, God, take me! We shall be near,
  More near than ever, each to each:
Her angel ears will find more clear
  My heavenly than my earthly speech;
And still, as I draw nigh to thee,
Her soul and mine shall closer be.

THE HERITAGE

THE rich man's son inherits lands,
   And piles of brick and stone, and gold,
And he inherits soft white hands,
   And tender flesh that fears the cold,
   Nor dares to wear a garment old ;
A heritage, it seems to me,
One scarce would wish to hold in fee.

The rich man's son inherits cares ;
   The bank may break, the factory burn,
A breath may burst his bubble shares,
   And soft white hands could hardly earn
   A living that would serve his turn ;
A heritage, it seems to me,
One scarce would wish to hold in fee.

The rich man's son inherits wants,
   His stomach craves for dainty fare ;
With sated heart he hears the pants
   Of toiling hinds with brown arms bare,
   And wearies in his easy-chair ;
A heritage, it seems to me,
One scarce would wish to hold in fee.

What doth the poor man's son inherit ?
   Stout muscles and a sinewy heart,
A hardy frame, a hardier spirit ;
   King of two hands, he does his part
   In every useful toil and art ;

A heritage, it seems to me,
A king might wish to hold in fee.

What doth the poor man's son inherit?
  Wishes o'erjoyed with humble things,
A rank adjudged by toil-won merit,
  Content that from employment springs,
  A heart that in his labor sings;
A heritage, it seems to me,
A king might wish to hold in fee.

What doth the poor man's son inherit?
  A patience learned of being poor,
Courage, if sorrow come, to bear it,
  A fellow feeling that is sure
  To make the outcast bless his door;
A heritage, it seems to me,
A king might wish to hold in fee.

O rich man's son! there is a toil
  That with all others level stands;
Large charity doth never soil,
  But only whiten, soft white hands;
  This is the best crop from thy lands,
A heritage, it seems to me,
Worth being rich to hold in fee.

O poor man's son! scorn not thy state;
  There is worse weariness than thine,
In merely being rich and great;
  Toil only gives the soul to shine,
  And makes rest fragrant and benign;

A heritage, it seems to me,
Worth being poor to hold in fee.

Both, heirs to some six feet of sod,
    Are equal in the earth at last;
Both, children of the same dear God,
    Prove title to your heirship vast
    By record of a well-filled past;
A heritage, it seems to me,
Well worth a life to hold in fee.

THE ROSE: A BALLAD

I

In his tower sat the poet
    Gazing on the roaring sea,
"Take this rose," he sighed, "and throw it
    Where there's none that loveth me.
On the rock the billow bursteth
    And sinks back into the seas,
But in vain my spirit thirsteth
    So to burst and be at ease.
Take, O sea! the tender blossom
    That hath lain against my breast;
On thy black and angry bosom
    It will find a surer rest.
Life is vain, and love is hollow,
    Ugly death stands there behind,
Hate and scorn and hunger follow
    Him that toileth for his kind."

I

Forth into the night he hurled it,
    And with bitter smile did mark
How the surly tempest whirled it
    Swift into the hungry dark.
Foam and spray drive back to leeward,
    And the gale, with dreary moan,
Drifts the helpless blossom seaward,
    Through the breakers all alone.

II

Stands a maiden, on the morrow,
    Musing by the wave-beat strand,
Half in hope and half in sorrow,
    Tracing words upon the sand:
" Shall I ever then behold him
    Who hath been my life so long,
Ever to this sick heart fold him,
    Be the spirit of his song?
Touch not, sea, the blessed letters
    I have traced upon thy shore,
Spare his name whose spirit fetters
    Mine with love forevermore ! "
Swells the tide and overflows it,
    But, with omen pure and meet,
Brings a little rose, and throws it
    Humbly at the maiden's feet.
Full of bliss she takes the token,
    And, upon her snowy breast,
Soothes the ruffled petals broken
    With the ocean's fierce unrest.

" Love is thine, O heart! and surely
    Peace shall also be thine own,
For the heart that trusteth purely
    Never long can pine alone."

III

In his tower sits the poet,
    Blisses new and strange to him
Fill his heart and overflow it
    With a wonder sweet and dim.
Up the beach the ocean slideth
    With a whisper of delight,
And the moon in silence glideth
    Through the peaceful blue of night.
Rippling o'er the poet's shoulder
    Flows a maiden's golden hair,
Maiden lips, with love grown bolder,
    Kiss his moon-lit forehead bare.
" Life is joy, and love is power,
    Death all fetters doth unbind,
Strength and wisdom only flower
    When we toil for all our kind.
Hope is truth, — the future giveth
    More than present takes away,
And the soul forever liveth
    Nearer God from day to day."
Not a word the maiden uttered,
    Fullest hearts are slow to speak,
But a withered rose-leaf fluttered
    Down upon the poet's cheek.

SONG

VIOLET! sweet violet!
Thine eyes are full of tears;
    Are they wet
    Even yet
With the thought of other years?
Or with gladness are they full,
For the night so beautiful,
And longing for those far-off spheres?

Loved one of my youth thou wast,
Of my merry youth,
    And I see,
    Tearfully,
All the fair and sunny past,
All its openness and truth,
Ever fresh and green in thee
As the moss is in the sea.

Thy little heart, that hath with love
Grown colored like the sky above,
On which thou lookest ever, —
    Can it know
    All the woe
Of hope for what returneth never,
All the sorrow and the longing
To these hearts of ours belonging?

    Out on it ! no foolish pining
        For the sky
        Dims thine eye,
Or for the stars so calmly shining;
Like thee let this soul of mine
Take hue from that wherefor I long,
Self-stayed and high, serene and strong,
Not satisfied with hoping — but divine.

    Violet ! dear violet !
    Thy blue eyes are only wet
With joy and love of Him who sent thee,
And for the fulfilling sense
Of that glad obedience
Which made thee all that Nature meant thee !

ROSALINE

Thou look'dst on me all yesternight,
Thine eyes were blue, thy hair was bright
As when we murmured our troth-plight
Beneath the thick stars, Rosaline !
Thy hair was braided on thy head,
As on the day we two were wed,
Mine eyes scarce knew if thou wert dead,
But my shrunk heart knew, Rosaline !

The death-watch ticked behind the wall,
The blackness rustled like a pall,

The moaning wind did rise and fall
Among the bleak pines, Rosaline!
My heart beat thickly in mine ears:
The lids may shut out fleshly fears,
But still the spirit sees and hears,
Its eyes are lidless, Rosaline!

A wildness rushing suddenly,
A knowing some ill shape is nigh,
A wish for death, a fear to die,
Is not this vengeance, Rosaline?
A loneliness that is not lone,
A love quite withered up and gone,
A strong soul ousted from its throne,
What wouldst thou further, Rosaline?

'T is drear such moonless nights as these,
Strange sounds are out upon the breeze,
And the leaves shiver in the trees,
And then thou comest, Rosaline!
I seem to hear the mourners go,
With long black garments trailing slow,
And plumes anodding to and fro,
As once I heard them, Rosaline!

Thy shroud is all of snowy white,
And, in the middle of the night,
Thou standest moveless and upright,
Gazing upon me, Rosaline!
There is no sorrow in thine eyes,
But evermore that meek surprise, —
O God! thy gentle spirit tries
To deem me guiltless, Rosaline!

Above thy grave the robin sings,
And swarms of bright and happy things
Flit all about with sunlit wings,
But I am cheerless, Rosaline!
The violets on the hillock toss,
The gravestone is o'ergrown with moss;
For Nature feels not any loss,
But I am cheerless, Rosaline!

I did not know when thou wast dead;
A blackbird whistling overhead
Thrilled through my brain; I would have fled,
But dared not leave thee, Rosaline!
The sun rolled down, and very soon,
Like a great fire, the awful moon
Rose, stained with blood, and then a swoon
Crept chilly o'er me, Rosaline!

The stars came out; and, one by one,
Each angel from his silver throne
Looked down and saw what I had done:
I dared not hide me, Rosaline!
I crouched; I feared thy corpse would cry
Against me to God's silent sky,
I thought I saw the blue lips try
To utter something, Rosaline!

I waited with a maddened grin
To hear that voice all icy thin
Slide forth and tell my deadly sin
To hell and heaven, Rosaline!
But no voice came, and then it seemed,
That, if the very corpse had screamed,

The sound like sunshine glad had streamed
Through that dark stillness, Rosaline!

And then, amid the silent night,
I screamed with horrible delight,
And in my brain an awful light
Did seem to crackle, Rosaline!
It is my curse! sweet memories fall
From me like snow, and only all
Of that one night, like cold worms, crawl
My doomed heart over, Rosaline!

Why wilt thou haunt me with thine eyes,
Wherein such blessed memories,
Such pitying forgiveness lies,
Than hate more bitter, Rosaline!
Woe 's me! I know that love so high
As thine, true soul, could never die,
And with mean clay in churchyard lie, —
Would it might be so, Rosaline!

A REQUIEM

Ay, pale and silent maiden,
    Cold as thou liest there,
Thine was the sunniest nature
    That ever drew the air;
The wildest and most wayward,
    And yet so gently kind,
Thou seemedst but to body
    A breath of summer wind.

Into the eternal shadow
   That girds our life around,
Into the infinite silence
   Wherewith Death's shore is bound,
Thou hast gone forth, belovëd !
   And I were mean to weep,
That thou hast left Life's shallows,
   And dost possess the Deep.

Thou liest low and silent,
   Thy heart is cold and still,
Thine eyes are shut forever,
   And Death hath had his will;
He loved and would have taken,
   I loved and would have kept,
We strove, — and he was stronger,
   And I have never wept.

Let him possess thy body,
   Thy soul is still with me,
More sunny and more gladsome
   Than it was wont to be :
Thy body was a fetter
   That bound me to the flesh,
Thank God that it is broken,
   And now I live afresh !

Now I can see thee clearly;
   The dusky cloud of clay,
That hid thy starry spirit,
   Is rent and blown away :

To earth I give thy body,
    Thy spirit to the sky,
I saw its bright wings growing,
    And knew that thou must fly.

Now I can love thee truly,
    For nothing comes between
The senses and the spirit,
    The seen and the unseen;
Lifts the eternal shadow,
    The silence bursts apart,
And the soul's boundless future
    Is present in my heart.

A PARABLE

WORN and footsore was the Prophet,
    When he gained the holy hill;
" God has left the earth," he murmured,
    " Here his presence lingers still.

" God of all the olden prophets,
    Wilt thou speak with men no more?
Have I not as truly served thee
    As thy chosen ones of yore?

" Hear me, guider of my fathers,
    Lo! a humble heart is mine;
By thy mercy I beseech thee
    Grant thy servant but a sign!"

Bowing then his head, he listened
    For an answer to his prayer;
No loud burst of thunder followed,
    Not a murmur stirred the air:

But the tuft of moss before him
    Opened while he waited yet,
And, from out the rock's hard bosom,
    Sprang a tender violet.

" God ! I thank thee," said the Prophet;
    " Hard of heart and blind was I,
Looking to the holy mountain
    For the gift of prophecy.

" Still thou speakest with thy children
    Freely as in eld sublime;
Humbleness, and love, and patience,
    Still give empire over time.

" Had I trusted in my nature,
    And had faith in lowly things,
Thou thyself wouldst then have sought me,
    And set free my spirit's wings.

" But I looked for signs and wonders,
    That o'er men should give me sway;
Thirsting to be more than mortal,
    I was even less than clay.

" Ere I entered on my journey,
    As I girt my loins to start,
Ran to me my little daughter,
    The belovëd of my heart;

"In her hand she held a flower,
    Like to this as like may be,
Which, beside my very threshold,
    She had plucked and brought to me."

SONG

O MOONLIGHT deep and tender,
    A year and more agone,
Your mist of golden splendor
    Round my betrothal shone!

O elm-leaves dark and dewy,
    The very same ye seem,
The low wind trembles through ye,
    Ye murmur in my dream!

O river, dim with distance,
    Flow thus forever by,
A part of my existence
    Within your heart doth lie!

O stars, ye saw our meeting,
    Two beings and one soul,
Two hearts so madly beating
    To mingle and be whole!

O happy night, deliver
    Her kisses back to me,
Or keep them all, and give her
    A blissful dream of me!

SONNETS

I

TO A. C. L.

THROUGH suffering and sorrow thou hast passed
To show us what a woman true may be :
They have not taken sympathy from thee,
Nor made thee any other than thou wast,
Save as some tree, which, in a sudden blast,
Sheddeth those blossoms, that are weakly grown,
Upon the air, but keepeth every one
Whose strength gives warrant of good fruit at last.
So thou hast shed some blooms of gayety,
But never one of steadfast cheerfulness ;
Nor hath thy knowledge of adversity
Robbed thee of any faith in happiness,
But rather cleared thine inner eyes to see
How many simple ways there are to bliss.

II

WHAT were I, Love, if I were stripped of thee,
If thine eyes shut me out whereby I live,
Thou, who unto my calmer soul dost give
Knowledge, and Truth, and holy Mystery,
Wherein Truth mainly lies for those who see
Beyond the earthly and the fugitive,
Who in the grandeur of the soul believe,
And only in the Infinite are free ?

Without thee I were naked, bleak, and bare
As yon dead cedar on the sea-cliff's brow;
And Nature's teachings, which come to me now,
Common and beautiful as light and air,
Would be as fruitless as a stream which still
Slips through the wheel of some old ruined mill.

III

I WOULD not have this perfect love of ours
Grow from a single root, a single stem,
Bearing no goodly fruit, but only flowers
That idly hide life's iron diadem:
It should grow alway like that Eastern tree
Whose limbs take root and spread forth constantly;
That love for one, from which there doth not spring
Wide love for all, is but a worthless thing.
Not in another world, as poets prate,
Dwell we apart above the tide of things,
High floating o'er earth's clouds on faery wings;
But our pure love doth ever elevate
Into a holy bond of brotherhood
All earthly things, making them pure and good.

IV

" FOR this true nobleness I seek in vain,
In woman and in man I find it not;
I almost weary of my earthly lot,
My life-springs are dried up with burning pain."
Thou find'st it not? I pray thee look again,
Look *inward* through the depths of thine own soul.
How is it with thee? Art thou sound and whole?

Doth narrow search show thee no earthly stain?
BE NOBLE! and the nobleness that lies
In other men, sleeping, but never dead,
Will rise in majesty to meet thine own ;
Then wilt thou see it gleam in many eyes,
Then will pure light around thy path be shed,
And thou wilt nevermore be sad and lone.

V

TO THE SPIRIT OF KEATS

GREAT soul, thou sittest with me in my room,
Uplifting me with thy vast, quiet eyes,
On whose full orbs, with kindly lustre, lies
The twilight warmth of ruddy ember-gloom :
Thy clear, strong tones will oft bring sudden bloom
Of hope secure, to him who lonely cries,
Wrestling with the young poet's agonies,
Neglect and scorn, which seem a certain doom :
Yes! the few words which, like great thunder-
        drops,
Thy large heart down to earth shook doubtfully,
Thrilled by the inward lightning of its might,
Serene and pure, like gushing joy of light,
Shall track the eternal chords of Destiny,
After the moon-led pulse of ocean stops.

VI

GREAT Truths are portions of the soul of man ;
Great souls are portions of Eternity ;

Each drop of blood that e'er through true heart ran
With lofty message, ran for thee and me;
For God's law, since the starry song began,
Hath been, and still forevermore must be,
That every deed which shall outlast Time's span
Must spur the soul to be erect and free;
Slave is no word of deathless lineage sprung;
Too many noble souls have thought and died,
Too many mighty poets lived and sung,
And our good Saxon, from lips purified
With martyr-fire, throughout the world hath rung
Too long to have God's holy cause denied.

VII

I ASK not for those thoughts, that sudden leap
From being's sea, like the isle-seeming Kraken,
With whose great rise the ocean all is shaken
And a heart-tremble quivers through the deep;
Give me that growth which some perchance deem
     sleep,
Wherewith the steadfast coral-stems uprise,
Which, by the toil of gathering energies,
Their upward way into clear sunshine keep,
Until, by Heaven's sweetest influences,
Slowly and slowly spreads a speck of green
Into a pleasant island in the seas,
Where, mid tall palms, the cane-roofed home is
     seen,
And wearied men shall sit at sunset's hour,
Hearing the leaves and loving God's dear power.

VIII

TO M. W., ON HER BIRTHDAY

Maiden, when such a soul as thine is born,
The morning-stars their ancient music make,
And, joyful, once again their song awake,
Long silent now with melancholy scorn;
And thou, not mindless of so blest a morn,
By no least deed its harmony shalt break,
But shalt to that high chime thy footsteps take,
Through life's most darksome passes unforlorn;
Therefore from thy pure faith thou shalt not fall,
Therefore shalt thou be ever fair and free,
And in thine every motion musical
As summer air, majestic as the sea,
A mystery to those who creep and crawl
Through Time, and part it from Eternity.

IX

My Love, I have no fear that thou shouldst die;
Albeit I ask no fairer life than this,
Whose numbering-clock is still thy gentle kiss,
While Time and Peace with hands enlockëd fly;
Yet care I not where in Eternity
We live and love, well knowing that there is
No backward step for those who feel the bliss
Of Faith as their most lofty yearnings high:
Love hath so purified my being's core,
Meseems I scarcely should be startled, even,
To find, some morn, that thou hadst gone before;

I

Since, with thy love, this knowledge too was given,
Which each calm day doth strengthen more and
      more,
That they who love are but one step from Heaven.

X

I CANNOT think that thou shouldst pass away,
Whose life to mine is an eternal law,
A piece of Nature that can have no flaw,
A new and certain sunrise every day;
But, if thou art to be another ray
About the Sun of Life, and art to live
Free from what part of thee was fugitive,
The debt of Love I will more fully pay,
Not downcast with the thought of thee so high,
But rather raised to be a nobler man,
And more divine in my humanity,
As knowing that the waiting eyes which scan
My life are lighted by a purer being,
And ask high, calm-browed deeds, with it agreeing.

XI

THERE never yet was flower fair in vain,
Let classic poets rhyme it as they will;
The seasons toil that it may blow again,
And summer's heart doth feel its every ill;
Nor is a true soul ever born for naught;
Wherever any such hath lived and died,
There hath been something for true freedom wrought,
Some bulwark levelled on the evil side:

Toil on, then, Greatness! thou art in the right,
However narrow souls may call thee wrong;
Be as thou wouldst be in thine own clear sight,
And so thou shalt be in the world's ere long;
For worldlings cannot, struggle as they may,
From man's great soul one great thought hide
    away.

XII

SUB PONDERE CRESCIT

THE hope of Truth grows stronger, day by day;
I hear the soul of Man around me waking,
Like a great sea, its frozen fetters breaking,
And flinging up to heaven its sunlit spray,
Tossing huge continents in scornful play,
And crushing them, with din of grinding thunder,
That makes old emptinesses stare in wonder;
The memory of a glory passed away
Lingers in every heart, as, in the shell,
Resounds the bygone freedom of the sea,
And every hour new signs of promise tell,
That the great soul shall once again be free,
For high, and yet more high, the murmurs swell
Of inward strife for truth and liberty.

XIII

BELOVED, in the noisy city here,
The thought of thee can make all turmoil cease;
Around my spirit, folds thy spirit clear
Its still, soft arms, and circles it with peace;

There is no room for any doubt or fear
In souls so overfilled with love's increase,
There is no memory of the bygone year
But growth in heart's and spirit's perfect ease:
How hath our love, half nebulous at first,
Rounded itself into a full-orbed sun!
How have our lives and wills (as haply erst
They were, ere this forgetfulness begun)
Through all their earthly distances outburst,
And melted, like two rays of light in one!

XIV

ON READING WORDSWORTH'S SONNETS IN DEFENCE OF
CAPITAL PUNISHMENT

As the broad ocean endlessly upheaveth,
With the majestic beating of his heart,
The mighty tides, whereof its rightful part
Each sea-wide bay and little weed receiveth,
So, through his soul who earnestly believeth,
Life from the universal Heart doth flow,
Whereby some conquest of the eternal Woe,
By instinct of God's nature, he achieveth:
A fuller pulse of this all-powerful beauty
Into the poet's gulf-like heart doth tide,
And he more keenly feels the glorious duty
Of serving Truth, despised and crucified, —
Happy, unknowing sect or creed, to rest,
And feel God flow forever through his breast.

XV

THE SAME CONTINUED

Once hardly in a cycle blossometh
A flower-like soul ripe with the seeds of song,
A spirit foreordained to cope with wrong,
Whose divine thoughts are natural as breath,
Who the old Darkness thickly scattereth
With starry words, that shoot prevailing light
Into the deeps, and wither, with the blight
Of serene Truth, the coward heart of Death:
Woe, if such spirit thwart its errand high,
And mock with lies the longing soul of man!
Yet one age longer must true Culture lie,
Soothing her bitter fetters as she can,
Until new messages of love outstart
At the next beating of the infinite Heart.

XVI

THE SAME CONTINUED

The love of all things springs from love of one;
Wider the soul's horizon hourly grows,
And over it with fuller glory flows
The sky-like spirit of God; a hope begun
In doubt and darkness 'neath a fairer sun
Cometh to fruitage, if it be of Truth;
And to the law of meekness, faith, and ruth,
By inward sympathy, shall all be won:
This thou shouldst know, who, from the painted
    feature

Of shifting Fashion, couldst thy brethren turn
Unto the love of ever-youthful Nature,
And of a beauty fadeless and eterne;
And always 't is the saddest sight to see
An old man faithless in Humanity.

XVII

THE SAME CONTINUED

A POET cannot strive for despotism;
His harp falls shattered; for it still must be
The instinct of great spirits to be free,
And the sworn foes of cunning barbarism:
He who has deepest searched the wide abysm
Of that life-giving Soul which men call fate,
Knows that to put more faith in lies and hate
Than truth and love is the true atheism:
Upward the soul forever turns her eyes:
The next hour always shames the hour before;
One beauty, at its highest, prophesies
That by whose side it shall seem mean and poor;
No Godlike thing knows aught of less and less,
But widens to the boundless Perfectness.

XVIII

THE SAME CONTINUED

THEREFORE think not the Past is wise alone,
For Yesterday knows nothing of the Best,
And thou shalt love it only as the nest
Whence glory-wingèd things to Heaven have flown:

To the great Soul only are all things known;
Present and future are to her as past,
While she in glorious madness doth forecast
That perfect bud, which seems a flower full-blown
To each new Prophet, and yet always opes
Fuller and fuller with each day and hour,
Heartening the soul with odor of fresh hopes,
And longings high, and gushings of wide power,
Yet never is or shall be fully blown
Save in the forethought of the Eternal One.

XIX

THE SAME CONCLUDED.

FAR 'yond this narrow parapet of Time,
With eyes uplift, the poet's soul should look
Into the Endless Promise, nor should brook
One prying doubt to shake his faith sublime;
To him the earth is ever in her prime
And dewiness of morning; he can see
Good lying hid, from all eternity,
Within the teeming womb of sin and crime;
His soul should not be cramped by any bar,
His nobleness should be so Godlike high,
That his least deed is perfect as a star,
His common look majestic as the sky,
And all o'erflooded with a light from far,
Undimmed by clouds of weak mortality.

XX

TO M. O. S.

MARY, since first I knew thee, to this hour,
My love hath deepened, with my wiser sense
Of what in Woman is to reverence;
Thy clear heart, fresh as e'er was forest-flower,
Still opens more to me its beauteous dower; —
But let praise hush, — Love asks no evidence
To prove itself well-placed; we know not whence
It gleans the straws that thatch its humble bower:
We can but say we found it in the heart,
Spring of all sweetest thoughts, arch foe of blame,
Sower of flowers in the dusty mart,
Pure vestal of the poet's holy flame, —
This is enough, and we have done our part
If we but keep it spotless as it came.

XXI

OUR love is not a fading, earthly flower:
Its wingèd seed dropped down from Paradise,
And, nursed by day and night, by sun and shower,
Doth momently to fresher beauty rise:
To us the leafless autumn is not bare,
Nor winter's rattling boughs lack lusty green.
Our summer hearts make summer's fulness, where
No leaf, or bud, or blossom may be seen:
For Nature's life in love's deep life doth lie,
Love, — whose forgetfulness is beauty's death, —

Whose mystic key these cells of Thou and I
Into the infinite freedom openeth,
And makes the body's dark and narrow grate
The wide-flung leaves of Heaven's own palace-gate.

XXII

IN ABSENCE

THESE rugged, wintry days I scarce could bear,
Did I not know, that, in the early spring,
When wild March winds upon their errands sing,
Thou wouldst return, bursting on this still air,
Like those same winds, when, startled from their lair,
They hunt up violets, and free swift brooks
From icy cares, even as thy clear looks
Bid my heart bloom, and sing, and break all care:
When drops with welcome rain the April day,
My flowers shall find their April in thine eyes,
Save there the rain in dreamy clouds doth stay,
As loath to fall out of those happy skies;
Yet sure, my love, thou art most like to May,
That comes with steady sun when April dies.

XXIII

WENDELL PHILLIPS

HE stood upon the world's broad threshold; wide
The din of battle and of slaughter rose;
He saw God stand upon the weaker side,
That sank in seeming loss before its foes:

Many there were who made great haste and sold
Unto the cunning enemy their swords,
He scorned their gifts of fame, and power, and
            gold,
And, underneath their soft and flowery words,
Heard the cold serpent hiss; therefore he went
And humbly joined him to the weaker part,
Fanatic named, and fool, yet well content
So he could be the nearer to God's heart,
And feel its solemn pulses sending blood
Through all the widespread veins of endless good.

XXIV

THE STREET

THEY pass me by like shadows, crowds on crowds,
Dim ghosts of men, that hover to and fro,
Hugging their bodies round them like thin shrouds
Wherein their souls were buried long ago:
They trampled on their youth, and faith, and love,
They cast their hope of human-kind away,
With Heaven's clear messages they madly strove,
And conquered, — and their spirits turned to clay:
Lo! how they wander round the world, their
            grave,
Whose ever-gaping maw by such is fed,
Gibbering at living men, and idly rave,
" We, only, truly live, but ye are dead."
Alas! poor fools, the anointed eye may trace
A dead soul's epitaph in every face!

XXV

I GRIEVE not that ripe Knowledge takes away
The charm that Nature to my childhood wore,
For, with that insight, cometh, day by day,
A greater bliss than wonder was before;
The real doth not clip the poet's wings, —
To win the secret of a weed's plain heart
Reveals some clue to spiritual things,
And stumbling guess becomes firm-footed art:
Flowers are not flowers unto the poet's eyes,
Their beauty thrills him by an inward sense;
He knows that outward seemings are but lies,
Or, at the most, but earthly shadows, whence
The soul that looks within for truth may guess
The presence of some wondrous heavenliness.

XXVI

TO J. R. GIDDINGS

GIDDINGS, far rougher names than thine have grown
Smoother than honey on the lips of men;
And thou shalt aye be honorably known,
As one who bravely used his tongue and pen,
As best befits a freeman, — even for those
To whom our Law's unblushing front denies
A right to plead against the lifelong woes
Which are the Negro's glimpse of Freedom's skies:
Fear nothing, and hope all things, as the Right
Alone may do securely; every hour

The thrones of Ignorance and ancient Night
Lose somewhat of their long-usurpëd power,
And Freedom's lightest word can make them shiver
With a base dread that clings to them forever.

XXVII

I THOUGHT our love at full, but I did err;
Joy's wreath drooped o'er mine eyes; I could not see
That sorrow in our happy world must be
Love's deepest spokesman and interpreter:
But, as a mother feels her child first stir
Under her heart, so felt I instantly
Deep in my soul another bond to thee
Thrill with that life we saw depart from her;
O mother of our angel child! twice dear!
Death knits as well as parts, and still, I wis,
Her tender radiance shall infold us here,
Even as the light, borne up by inward bliss,
Threads the void glooms of space without a fear,
To print on farthest stars her pitying kiss.

L'ENVOI

WHETHER my heart hath wiser grown or not,
In these three years, since I to thee inscribed,
Mine own betrothed, the firstlings of my muse, —
Poor windfalls of unripe experience,
Young buds plucked hastily by childish hands
Not patient to await more full-blown flowers, —
At least it hath seen more of life and men,

And pondered more, and grown a shade more sad ;
Yet with no loss of hope or settled trust
In the benignness of that Providence
Which shapes from out our elements awry
The grace and order that we wonder at,
The mystic harmony of right and wrong,
Both working out His wisdom and our good :
A trust, Beloved, chiefly learned of thee,
Who hast that gift of patient tenderness,
The instinctive wisdom of a woman's heart.

They tell us that our land was made for song,
With its huge rivers and sky-piercing peaks,
Its sealike lakes and mighty cataracts,
Its forests vast and hoar, and prairies wide,
And mounds that tell of wondrous tribes extinct.
But Poesy springs not from rocks and woods ;
Her womb and cradle are the human heart,
And she can find a nobler theme for song
In the most loathsome man that blasts the sight
Than in the broad expanse of sea and shore
Between the frozen deserts of the poles.
All nations have their message from on high,
Each the messiah of some central thought,
For the fulfilment and delight of Man :
One has to teach that labor is divine ;
Another Freedom ; and another Mind ;
And all, that God is open-eyed and just,
The happy centre and calm heart of all.

Are, then, our woods, our mountains, and our streams,
Needful to teach our poets how to sing ?

O maiden rare, far other thoughts were ours,
When we have sat by ocean's foaming marge,
And watched the waves leap roaring on the rocks,
Than young Leander and his Hero had,
Gazing from Sestos to the other shore.
The moon looks down and ocean worships her,
Stars rise and set, and seasons come and go
Even as they did in Homer's elder time,
But we behold them not with Grecian eyes :
Then they were types of beauty and of strength,
But now of freedom, unconfined and pure,
Subject alone to Order's higher law.
What cares the Russian serf or Southern slave
Though we should speak as man spake never yet
Of gleaming Hudson's broad magnificence,
Or green Niagara's never-ending roar ?
Our country hath a gospel of her own
To preach and practise before all the world, —
The freedom and divinity of man,
The glorious claims of human brotherhood, —
Which to pay nobly, as a freeman should,
Gains the sole wealth that will not fly away, —
And the soul's fealty to none but God.
These are realities, which make the shows
Of outward Nature, be they ne'er so grand,
Seem small, and worthless, and contemptible.
These are the mountain-summits for our bards,
Which stretch far upward into Heaven itself,
And give such widespread and exulting view
Of hope, and faith, and onward destiny,
That shrunk Parnassus to a molehill dwindles.
Our new Atlantis, like a morning-star,

Silvers the mirk face of slow-yielding Night,
The herald of a fuller truth than yet
Hath gleamed upon the upraised face of Man
Since the earth glittered in her stainless prime, —
Of a more glorious sunrise than of old
Drew wondrous melodies from Memnon huge,
Yea, draws them still, though now he sit waist-deep
In the ingulfing flood of whirling sand,
And look across the wastes of endless gray,
Sole wreck, where once his hundred-gated Thebes
Pained with her mighty hum the calm, blue heaven:
Shall the dull stone pay grateful orisons,
And we till noonday bar the splendor out,
Lest it reproach and chide our sluggard hearts,
Warm-nestled in the down of Prejudice,
And be content, though clad with angel-wings,
Close-clipped, to hop about from perch to perch,
In paltry cages of dead men's dead thoughts?
Oh, rather, like the skylark, soar and sing,
And let our gushing songs befit the dawn
And sunrise, and the yet unshaken dew
Brimming the chalice of each full-blown hope,
Whose blithe front turns to greet the growing day!
Never had poets such high call before,
Never can poets hope for higher one,
And, if they be but faithful to their trust,
Earth will remember them with love and joy,
And oh, far better, God will not forget.
For he who settles Freedom's principles
Writes the death-warrant of all tyranny;
Who speaks the truth stabs Falsehood to the heart,
And his mere word makes despots tremble more

Than ever Brutus with his dagger could.
Wait for no hints from waterfalls or woods,
Nor dream that tales of red men, brute and fierce,
Repay the finding of this Western World,
Or needed half the globe to give them birth :
Spirit supreme of Freedom ! not for this
Did great Columbus tame his eagle soul
To jostle with the daws that perch in courts ;
Not for this, friendless, on an unknown sea,
Coping with mad waves and more mutinous spirits,
Battled he with the dreadful ache at heart
Which tempts, with devilish subtleties of doubt,
The hermit of that loneliest solitude,
The silent desert of a great New Thought ;
Though loud Niagara were to-day struck dumb,
Yet would this cataract of boiling life
Rush plunging on and on to endless deeps,
And utter thunder till the world shall cease, —
A thunder worthy of the poet's song,
And which alone can fill it with true life.
The high evangel to our country granted
Could make apostles, yea, with tongues of fire,
Of hearts half-darkened back again to clay !
'T is the soul only that is national,
And he who pays true loyalty to that
Alone can claim the wreath of patriotism.

Beloved ! if I wander far and oft
From that which I believe, and feel, and know,
Thou wilt forgive, not with a sorrowing heart,
But with a strengthened hope of better things ;
Knowing that I, though often blind and false

To those I love, and oh, more false than all
Unto myself, have been most true to thee,
And that whoso in one thing hath been true
Can be as true in all. Therefore thy hope
May yet not prove unfruitful, and thy love
Meet, day by day, with less unworthy thanks,
Whether, as now, we journey hand in hand,
Or, parted in the body, yet are one
In spirit and the love of holy things.

MISCELLANEOUS POEMS

A LEGEND OF BRITTANY

PART FIRST

I

FAIR as a summer dream was Margaret,
  Such dream as in a poet's soul might start,
Musing of old loves while the moon doth set .
  Her hair was not more sunny than her heart,
Though like a natural golden coronet
  It circled her dear head with careless art,
Mocking the sunshine, that would fain have lent
To its frank grace a richer ornament.

II

His lóved one's eyes could poet ever speak,
  So kind, so dewy, and so deep were hers, —
But, while he strives, the choicest phrase, too weak,
  Their glad reflection in his spirit blurs ;
As one may see a dream dissolve and break
  Out of his grasp when he to tell it stirs,
Like that sad Dryad doomed no more to bless
The mortal who revealed her loveliness.

III

She dwelt forever in a region bright,
  Peopled with living fancies of her own,
Where naught could come but visions of delight,
  Far, far aloof from earth's eternal moan :

A summer cloud thrilled through with rosy light,
  Floating beneath the blue sky all alone,
Her spirit wandered by itself, and won
A golden edge from some unsetting sun.

IV ·

The heart grows richer that its lot is poor,
  God blesses want with larger sympathies,
Love enters gladliest at the humble door,
  And makes the cot a palace with his eyes ;
So Margaret's heart a softer beauty wore,
  And grew in gentleness and patience wise,
For she was but a simple herdsman's child,
A lily chance-sown in the rugged wild.

V

There was no beauty of the wood or field
  But she its fragrant bosom-secret knew,
Nor any but to her would freely yield
  Some grace that in her soul took root and grew :
Nature to her shone as but now revealed,
  All rosy-fresh with innocent morning dew,
And looked into her heart with dim, sweet eyes
That left it full of sylvan memories.

VI

Oh, what a face was hers to brighten light,
  And give back sunshine with an added glow,
To wile each moment with a fresh delight,
  And part of memory's best contentment grow !
Oh, how her voice, as with an inmate's right,
  Into the strangest heart would welcome go,

And make it sweet, and ready to become
Of white and gracious thoughts the chosen home !

VII

None looked upon her but he straightway thought
    Of all the greenest depths of country cheer,
And into each one's heart was freshly brought
    What was to him the sweetest time of year,
So was her every look and motion fraught
    With out-of-door delights and forest lere ;
Not the first violet on a woodland lea
Seemed a more visible gift of Spring than she.

VIII

Is love learned only out of poets' books ?
    Is there not somewhat in the dropping flood,
And in the nunneries of silent nooks,
    And in the murmured longing of the wood,
That could make Margaret dream of love-lorn looks,
    And stir a thrilling mystery in her blood
More trembly secret than Aurora's tear
Shed in the bosom of an eglatere ?

IX

Full many a sweet forewarning hath the mind,
    Full many a whispering of vague desire,
Ere comes the nature destined to unbind
    Its virgin zone, and all its deeps inspire, —
Low stirrings in the leaves, before the wind
    Wake all the green strings of the forest lyre,
Faint heatings in the calyx, ere the rose
Its warm voluptuous breast doth all unclose.

X

Long in its dim recesses pines the spirit,
    Wildered and dark, despairingly alone ;
Though many a shape of beauty wander near it,
    And many a wild and half-remembered tone
Tremble from the divine abyss to cheer it,
    Yet still it knows that there is only one
Before whom it can kneel and tribute bring,
At once a happy vassal and a king.

XI

To feel a want, yet scarce know what it is,
    To seek one nature that is always new,
Whose glance is warmer than another's kiss,
    Whom we can bare our inmost beauty to,
Nor feel deserted afterwards, — for this
    But with our destined co-mate we can do, —
Such longing instinct fills the mighty scope
Of the young soul with one mysterious hope.

XII

So Margaret's heart grew brimming with the lore
    Of love's enticing secrets ; and although
She had found none to cast it down before,
    Yet oft to Fancy's chapel she would go
To pay her vows, and count the rosary o'er
    Of her love's promised graces : — haply so
Miranda's hope had pictured Ferdinand
Long ere the gaunt wave tossed him on the strand.

XIII

A new-made star that swims the lonely gloom,
  Unwedded yet and longing for the sun,
Whose beams, the bride-gifts of the lavish groom,
  Blithely to crown the virgin planet run,
Her being was, watching to see the bloom
  Of love's fresh sunrise roofing one by one
Its clouds with gold, a triumph-arch to be
For him who came to hold her heart in fee. .

XIV

Not far from Margaret's cottage dwelt a knight
  Of the proud Templars, a sworn celibate,
Whose heart in secret fed upon the light
  And dew of her ripe beauty, through the grate
Of his close vow catching what gleams he might
  Of the free heaven, and cursing all too late
The cruel faith whose black walls hemmed him in
And turned life's crowning bliss to deadly sin.

XV

For he had met her in the wood by chance,
  And, having drunk her beauty's wildering spell,
His heart shook like the pennon of a lance
  That quivers in a breeze's sudden swell,
And thenceforth, in a close-infolded trance,
  From mistily golden deep to deep he fell;
Till earth did waver and fade far away
Beneath the hope in whose warm arms he lay.

XVI

A dark, proud man he was, whose half-blown youth
   Had shed its blossoms even in opening,
Leaving a few that with more winning ruth
     Trembling around grave manhood's stem might
       cling,
More sad than cheery, making, in good sooth,
   Like the fringed gentian, a late autumn spring:
A twilight nature, braided light and gloom,
A youth half-smiling by an open tomb.

XVII

Fair as an angel, who yet inly wore
   A wrinkled heart foreboding his near fall;
Who saw him alway wished to know him more,
   As if he were some fate's defiant thrall
And nursed a dreaded secret at his core;
   Little he loved, but power the most of all,
And that he seemed to scorn, as one who knew
By what foul paths men choose to crawl thereto.

XVIII

He had been noble, but some great deceit
   Had turned his better instinct to a vice:
He strove to think the world was all a cheat,
   That power and fame were cheap at any price,
That the sure way of being shortly great
   Was even to play life's game with loaded dice,
Since he had tried the honest play and found
That vice and virtue differed but in sound.

XIX

Yet Margaret's sight redeemed him for a space
   From his own thraldom; man could never be
A hypocrite when first such maiden grace
   Smiled in upon his heart; the agony
Of wearing all day long a lying face
   Fell lightly from him, and, a moment free,
Erect with wakened faith his spirit stood
And scorned the weakness of his demon-mood.

XX

Like a sweet wind-harp to him was her thought,
   Which would not let the common air come near,
Till from its dim enchantment it had caught
   A musical tenderness that brimmed his ear
With sweetness more ethereal than aught
   Save silver-dropping snatches that whilere
Rained down from some sad angel's faithful harp
To cool her fallen lover's anguish sharp.

XXI

Deep in the forest was a little dell
   High overarchëd with the leafy sweep
Of a broad oak, through whose gnarled roots there fell
   A slender rill that sung itself to sleep,
Where its continuous toil had scooped a well
   To please the fairy folk; breathlessly deep
The stillness was, save when the dreaming brook
From its small urn a drizzly murmur shook.

XXII

The wooded hills sloped upward all around
    With gradual rise, and made an even rim,
So that it seemed a mighty casque unbound
    From some huge Titan's brow to lighten him,
Ages ago and left upon the ground,
    Where the slow soil had mossed it to the brim,
Till after countless centuries it grew
Into this dell, the haunt of noontide dew.

XXIII

Dim vistas, sprinkled o'er with sun-flecked green,
    Wound through the thickset trunks on every side,
And, toward the west, in fancy might be seen
    A Gothic window in its blazing pride,
When the low sun, two arching elms between,
    Lit up the leaves beyond, which, autumn-dyed
With lavish hues, would into splendor start,
Shaming the labored panes of richest art.

XXIV

Here, leaning once against the old oak's trunk,
    Mordred, for such was the young Templar's name,
Saw Margaret come; unseen, the falcon shrunk
    From the meek dove; sharp thrills of tingling flame
Made him forget that he was vowed a monk,
    And all the outworks of his pride o'ercame:
Flooded he seemed with bright delicious pain,
As if a star had burst within his brain.

XXV

Such power hath beauty and frank innocence :
   A flower bloomed forth, that sunshine glad to bless,
Even from his love's long leafless stem ; the sense
   Of exile from Hope's happy realm grew less,
And thoughts of childish peace, he knew not whence,
   Thronged round his heart with many an old caress,
Melting the frost there into pearly dew
That mirrored back his nature's morning-blue.

XXVI

She turned and saw him, but she felt no dread,
   Her purity, like adamantine mail,
Did so encircle her ; and yet her head
   She drooped, and made her golden hair her veil,
Through which a glow of rosiest lustre spread,
   Then faded, and anon she stood all pale,
As snow o'er which a blush of northern-light
Suddenly reddens, and as soon grows white.

XXVII

She thought of Tristrem and of Lancilot,
   Of all her dreams, and of kind fairies' might,
And how that dell was deemed a haunted spot,
   Until there grew a mist before her sight,
And where the present was she half forgot,
   Borne backward through the realms of old de-
       light, —
Then, starting up awake, she would have gone,
Yet almost wished it might not be alone.

XXVIII

How they went home together through the wood,
 And how all life seemed focussed into one
Thought-dazzling spot that set ablaze the blood,
 What need to tell? Fit language there is none
For the heart's deepest things. Who ever wooed
 As in his boyish hope he would have done?
For, when the soul is fullest, the hushed tongue
Voicelessly trembles like a lute unstrung.

XXIX

But all things carry the heart's messages
 And know it not, nor doth the heart well know,
But Nature hath her will; even as the bees,
 Blithe go-betweens, fly singing to and fro
With the fruit-quickening pollen; — hard if these
 Found not some all unthought-of way to show
Their secret each to each; and so they did,
And one heart's flower-dust into the other slid.

XXX

Young hearts are free; the selfish world it is
 That turns them miserly and cold as stone,
And makes them clutch their fingers on the bliss
 Which but in giving truly is their own; —
She had no dreams of barter, asked not his,
 But gave hers freely as she would have thrown
A rose to him, or as that rose gives forth
Its generous fragrance, thoughtless of its worth.

XXXI

Her summer nature felt a need to bless,
    And a like longing to be blest again;
So, from her sky-like spirit, gentleness
    Dropt ever like a sunlit fall of rain,
And his beneath drank in the bright caress
    As thirstily as would a parchëd plain,
That long hath watched the showers of sloping gray
For ever, ever, falling far away.

XXXII

How should she dream of ill? the heart filled quite
    With sunshine, like the shepherd's-clock at noon,
Closes its leaves around its warm delight;
    Whate'er in life is harsh or out of tune
Is all shut out, no boding shade of blight
    Can pierce the opiate ether of its swoon:
Love is but blind as thoughtful justice is,
But naught can be so wanton-blind as bliss.

XXXIII

All beauty and all life he was to her;
    She questioned not his love, she only knew
That she loved him, and not a pulse could stir
    In her whole frame but quivered through and through
With this glad thought, and was a minister
    To do him fealty and service true,
Like golden ripples hasting to the land
To wreck their freight of sunshine on the strand.

XXXIV

O dewy dawn of love ! O hopes that are
   Hung high, like the cliff-swallow's perilous nest,
Most like to fall when fullest, and that jar
   With every heavier billow ! O unrest
Than balmiest deeps of quiet sweeter far !
   How did ye triumph now in Margaret's breast,
Making it readier to shrink and start
Than quivering gold of the pond-lily's heart !

XXXV

Here let us pause: oh, would the soul might ever
   Achieve its immortality in youth,
When nothing yet hath damped its high endeavor
   After the starry energy of truth !
Here let us pause, and for a moment sever
   This gleam of sunshine from the sad unruth
That sometime comes to all, for it is good
To lengthen to the last a sunny mood.

PART SECOND

I

As one who, from the sunshine and the green,
   Enters the solid darkness of a cave,
Nor knows what precipice or pit unseen
   May yawn before him with its sudden grave,
And, with hushed breath, doth often forward lean
   Dreaming he hears the plashing of a wave

Dimly below, or feels a damper air
From out some dreary chasm, he knows not where;

II

So, from the sunshine and the green of love,
   We enter on our story's darker part;
And, though the horror of it well may move
   An impulse of repugnance in the heart,
Yet let us think, that, as there 's naught above
   The all-embracing atmosphere of Art,
So also there is naught that falls below
Her generous reach, though grimed with guilt and woe.

III

Her fittest triumph is to show that good
   Lurks in the heart of evil evermore,
That love, though scorned, and outcast, and withstood,
   Can without end forgive, and yet have store;
God's love and man's are of the selfsame blood,
   And He can see that always at the door
Of foulest hearts the angel-nature yet
Knocks to return and cancel all its debt.

IV

It ever is weak falsehood's destiny
   That her thick mask turns crystal to let through
The unsuspicious eyes of honesty;
   But Margaret's heart was too sincere and true
Aught but plain truth and faithfulness to see,
   And Mordred's for a time a little grew
To be like hers, won by the mild reproof
Of those kind eyes that kept all doubt aloof.

I

V

Full oft they met, as dawn and twilight meet
   In northern climes ; she full of growing day
As he of darkness, which before her feet
   Shrank gradual, and faded quite away,
Soon to return ; for power had made love sweet
   To him, and, when his will had gained full sway,
The taste began to pall ; for never power
Can sate the hungry soul beyond an hour.

VI

He fell as doth the tempter ever fall,
   Even in the gaining of his loathsome end ;
God doth not work as man works, but makes all
   The crooked paths of ill to goodness tend ;
Let Him judge Margaret ! If to be the thrall
   Of love, and faith too generous to defend
Its very life from him she loved, be sin,
What hope of grace may the seducer win ?

VII

Grim-hearted world, that look'st with Levite eyes
   On those poor fallen by too much faith in man,
She that upon thy freezing threshold lies,
   Starved to more sinning by thy savage ban,
Seeking that refuge because foulest vice
   More Godlike than thy virtue is, whose span
Shuts out the wretched only, is more free
To enter heaven than thou shalt ever be !

VIII

Thou wilt not let her wash thy dainty feet
    With such salt things as tears, or with rude hair
Dry them, soft Pharisee, that sit'st at meat
    With him who made her such, and speak'st him fair,
Leaving God's wandering lamb the while to bleat
    Unheeded, shivering in the pitiless air:
Thou hast made prisoned virtue show more wan
And haggard than a vice to look upon.

IX

Now many months flew by, and weary grew
    To Margaret the sight of happy things;
Blight fell on all her flowers, instead of dew;
    Shut round her heart were now the joyous wings
Wherewith it wont to soar; yet not untrue,
    Though tempted much, her woman's nature clings
To its first pure belief, and with sad eyes
Looks backward o'er the gate of Paradise.

X

And so, though altered Mordred came less oft,
    And winter frowned where spring had laughed
        before
In his strange eyes, yet half her sadness doffed,
    And in her silent patience loved him more:
Sorrow had made her soft heart yet more soft,
    And a new life within her own she bore
Which made her tenderer, as she felt it move
Beneath her breast, a refuge for her love.

XI

This babe, she thought, would surely bring him back,
    And be a bond forever them between ;
Before its eyes the sullen tempest-rack
    Would fade, and leave the face of heaven serene ;
And love's return doth more than fill the lack,
    Which in his absence withered the heart's green :
And yet a dim foreboding still would flit
Between her and her hope to darken it.

XII

She could not figure forth a happy fate,
    Even for this life from heaven so newly come ;
The earth must needs be doubly desolate
    To him scarce parted from a fairer home :
Such boding heavier on her bosom sate
    One night, as, standing in the twilight gloam,
She strained her eyes beyond that dizzy verge
At whose foot faintly breaks the future's surge.

XIII

Poor little spirit ! naught but shame and woe
    Nurse the sick heart whose lifeblood nurses thine :
Yet not those only ; love hath triumphed so,
    As for thy sake makes sorrow more divine :
And yet, though thou be pure, the world is foe
    To purity, if born in such a shrine ;
And, having trampled it for struggling thence,
Smiles to itself, and calls it Providence.

XIV

As thus she mused, a shadow seemed to rise
  From out her thought, and turn to dreariness
All blissful hopes and sunny memories,
  And the quick blood would curdle up and press
About her heart, which seemed to shut its eyes
  And hush itself, as who with shuddering guess
Harks through the gloom and dreads e'en now to feel
Through his hot breast the icy slide of steel.

XV

But, at that heart-beat, while in dread she was,
  In the low wind the honeysuckles gleam,
A dewy thrill flits through the heavy grass,
  And, looking forth, she saw, as in a dream,
Within the wood the moonlight's shadowy mass:
  Night's starry heart yearning to hers doth seem,
And the deep sky, full-hearted with the moon,
Folds round her all the happiness of June.

XVI

What fear could face a heaven and earth like this?
  What silveriest cloud could hang 'neath such a
    sky?
A tide of wondrous and unwonted bliss
  Rolls back through all her pulses suddenly,
As if some seraph, who had learned to kiss
  From the fair daughters of the world gone by,
Had wedded so his fallen light with hers,
Such sweet, strange joy through soul and body stirs.

XVII

Now seek we Mordred: he who did not fear
    The crime, yet fears the latent consequence:
If it should reach a brother Templar's ear,
    It haply might be made a good pretence
To cheat him of the hope he held most dear;
    For he had spared no thought's or deed's ex-
        pense,
That by and by might help his wish to clip
Its darling bride, — the high grandmastership.

XVIII

The apathy, ere a crime resolved is done,
    Is scarce less dreadful than remorse for crime;
By no allurement can the soul be won
    From brooding o'er the weary creep of time:
Mordred stole forth into the happy sun,
    Striving to hum a scrap of Breton rhyme,
But the sky struck him speechless, and he tried
In vain to summon up his callous pride.

XIX

In the courtyard a fountain leaped alway,
    A Triton blowing jewels through his shell
Into the sunshine; Mordred turned away,
    Weary because the stone face did not tell
Of weariness, nor could he bear to-day,
    Heartsick, to hear the patient sink and swell
Of winds among the leaves, or golden bees
Drowsily humming in the orange-trees.

XX

All happy sights and sounds now came to him
   Like a reproach : he wandered far and wide,
Following the lead of his unquiet whim,
   But still there went a something at his side
That made the cool breeze hot, the sunshine dim;
   It would not flee, it could not be defied,
He could not see it, but he felt it there,
By the damp chill that crept among his hair.

XXI

Day wore at last ; the evening-star arose,
   And throbbing in the sky grew red and set ;
Then with a guilty, wavering step he goes
   To the hid nook where they so oft had met
In happier season, for his heart well knows
   That he is sure to find poor Margaret
Watching and waiting there with love-lorn breast
Around her young dream's rudely scattered nest.

XXII

Why follow here that grim old chronicle
Which counts the dagger-strokes and drops of
      blood ?
Enough that Margaret by his mad steel fell,
   Unmoved by murder from her trusting mood,
Smiling on him as Heaven smiles on Hell,
   With a sad love, remembering when he stood
Not fallen yet, the unsealer of her heart,
Of all her holy dreams the holiest part.

XXIII

His crime complete, scarce knowing what he did
    (So goes the tale), beneath the altar there
In the high church the stiffening corpse he hid,
    And then, to 'scape that suffocating air,
Like a scared ghoul out of the porch he slid;
    But his strained eyes saw blood-spots everywhere,
And ghastly faces thrust themselves between
His soul and hopes of peace with blasting mien.

XXIV

His heart went out within him like a spark
    Dropt in the sea; wherever he made bold
To turn his eyes, he saw, all stiff and stark,
    Pale Margaret lying dead; the lavish gold
Of her loose hair seemed in the cloudy dark
    To spread a glory, and a thousandfold
More strangely pale and beautiful she grew:
Her silence stabbed his conscience through and
        through.

XXV

Or visions of past days, — a mother's eyes
    That smiled down on the fair boy at her knee,
Whose happy upturned face to hers replies, —
    He saw sometimes: or Margaret mournfully
Gazed on him full of doubt, as one who tries
    To crush belief that does love injury;
Then she would wring her hands, but soon again
Love's patience glimmered out through cloudy pain.

XXVI

Meanwhile he dared not go and steal away
   The silent, dead-cold witness of his sin;
He had not feared the life, but that dull clay,
   Those open eyes that showed the death within,
Would surely stare him mad; yet all the day
   A dreadful impulse, whence his will could win
No refuge, made him linger in the aisle,
Freezing with his wan look each greeting smile.

XXVII

Now, on the second day there was to be
   A festival in church: from far and near
Came flocking in the sunburnt peasantry,
   And knights and dames with stately antique
       cheer,
Blazing with pomp, as if all faërie
   Had emptied her quaint halls, or, as it were,
The illuminated marge of some old book,
While we were gazing, life and motion took.

XXVIII

When all were entered, and the roving eyes
   Of all were stayed, some upon faces bright,
Some on the priests, some on the traceries
   That decked the slumber of a marble knight,
And all the rustlings over that arise
   From recognizing tokens of delight,
When friendly glances meet, — then silent ease
Spread o'er the multitude by slow degrees.

XXIX

Then swelled the organ : up through choir and nave
  The music trembled with an inward thrill
Of bliss at its own grandeur : wave on wave
  Its flood of mellow thunder rose, until
The hushed air shivered with the throb it gave,
  Then, poising for a moment, it stood still,
And sank and rose again, to burst in spray
That wandered into silence far away.

XXX

Like to a mighty heart the music seemed,
  That yearns with melodies it cannot speak,
Until, in grand despair of what it dreamed,
  In the agony of effort it doth break,
Yet triumphs breaking ; on it rushed and streamed
  And wantoned in its might, as when a lake,
Long pent among the mountains, bursts its walls
And in one crowding gush leaps forth and falls.

XXXI

Deeper and deeper shudders shook the air,
  As the huge bass kept gathering heavily,
Like thunder when it rouses in its lair,
  And with its hoarse growl shakes the low-hung sky,
It grew up like a darkness everywhere,
  Filling the vast cathedral ; — suddenly,
From the dense mass a boy's clear treble broke
Like lightning, and the full-toned choir awoke.

XXXII

Through gorgeous windows shone the sun aslant,
　　Brimming the church with gold and purple mist,
Meet atmosphere to bosom that rich chant,
　　Where fifty voices in one strand did twist
Their varicolored tones, and left no want
　　To the delighted soul, which sank abyssed
In the warm music cloud, while, far below,
The organ heaved its surges to and fro.

XXXIII

As if a lark should suddenly drop dead
　　While the blue air yet trembled with its song,
So snapped at once that music's golden thread,
　　Struck by a nameless fear that leapt along
From heart to heart, and like a shadow spread
　　With instantaneous shiver through the throng,
So that some glanced behind, as half aware
A hideous shape of dread were standing there.

XXXIV

As when a crowd of pale men gather round,
　　Watching an eddy in the leaden deep,
From which they deem the body of one drowned
　　Will be cast forth, from face to face doth creep
An eager dread that holds all tongues fast bound
　　Until the horror, with a ghastly leap,
Starts up, its dead blue arms stretched aimlessly,
Heaved with the swinging of the careless sea, —

XXXV

So in the faces of all these there grew,
    As by one impulse, a dark, freezing awe,
Which, with a fearful fascination drew
    All eyes toward the altar; damp and raw
The air grew suddenly, and no man knew
    Whether perchance his silent neighbor saw
The dreadful thing which all were sure would rise
To scare the strained lids wider from their eyes.

XXXVI

The incense trembled as it upward sent
    Its slow, uncertain thread of wandering blue,
As 't were the only living element
    In all the church, so deep the stillness grew;
It seemed one might have heard it, as it went,
    Give out an audible rustle, curling through
The midnight silence of that awestruck air,
More hushed than death, though so much life was
        there.

XXXVII

Nothing they saw, but a low voice was heard
    Threading the ominous silence of that fear,
Gentle and terrorless as if a bird,
    Wakened by some volcano's glare, should cheer
The mirk air with his song; yet every word
    In the cathedral's farthest arch seemed near,
As if it spoke to every one apart,
Like the clear voice of conscience in each heart.

XXXVIII

" O Rest, to weary hearts thou art most dear!
    O Silence, after life's bewildering din,
Thou art most welcome, whether in the sear
    Days of our age thou comest, or we win
Thy poppy-wreath in youth! then wherefore here
    Linger I yet, once free to enter in
At that wished gate which gentle Death doth ope,
Into the boundless realm of strength and hope?'

XXXIX

" Think not in death my love could ever cease;
    If thou wast false, more need there is for me
Still to be true; that slumber were not peace,
    If 't were unvisited with dreams of thee:
And thou hadst never heard such words as these,
    Save that in heaven I must forever be
Most comfortless and wretched, seeing this
Our unbaptizëd babe shut out from bliss.

XL

" This little spirit with imploring eyes
    Wanders alone the dreary wild of space;
The shadow of his pain forever lies
    Upon my soul in this new dwelling-place;
His loneliness makes me in Paradise
    More lonely, and, unless I see his face,
Even here for grief could I lie down and die,
Save for my curse of immortality.

XLI

" World after world he sees around him swim
    Crowded with happy souls, that take no heed
Of the sad eyes that from the night's faint rim
    Gaze sick with longing on them as they speed
With golden gates, that only shut on him ;
    And shapes sometimes from hell's abysses freed
Flap darkly by him, with enormous sweep
Of wings that roughen wide the pitchy deep.

XLII

" I am a mother, — spirits do not shake
    This much of earth from them, — and I must
      pine
Till I can feel his little hands, and take
    His weary head upon this heart of mine ;
And, might it be, full gladly for his sake
    Would I this solitude of bliss resign
And be shut out of heaven to dwell with him
Forever in that silence drear and dim.

XLIII

" I strove to hush my soul, and would not speak
    At first, for thy dear sake ; a woman's love
Is mighty, but a mother's heart is weak,
    And by its weakness overcomes ; I strove
To smother bitter thoughts with patience meek,
    But still in the abyss my soul would rove,
Seeking my child, and drove me here to claim
The rite that gives him peace in Christ's dear name.

XLIV

"I sit and weep while blessed spirits sing;
  I can but long and pine the while they praise,
And, leaning o'er the wall of heaven, I fling
  My voice to where I deem my infant strays,
Like a robbed bird that cries in vain to bring
  Her nestlings back beneath her wings' embrace;
But still he answers not, and I but know
That heaven and earth are both alike in woe."

XLV

Then the pale priests, with ceremony due,
  Baptized the child within its dreadful tomb
Beneath that mother's heart, whose instinct true
  Star-like had battled down the triple gloom
Of sorrow, love, and death: young maidens, too,
  Strewed the pale corpse with many a milkwhite
    bloom,
And parted the bright hair, and on the breast
Crossed the unconscious hands in sign of rest.

XLVI

Some said, that, when the priest had sprinkled o'er
  The consecrated drops, they seemed to hear
A sigh, as of some heart from travail sore
  Released, and then two voices singing clear,
Misereatur Deus, more and more
  Fading far upward, and their ghastly fear
Fell from them with that sound, as bodies fall
From souls upspringing to celestial hall.

PROMETHEUS

One after one the stars have risen and set,
Sparkling upon the hoarfrost on my chain:
The Bear, that prowled all night about the fold
Of the North-star, hath shrunk into his den,
Scared by the blithesome footsteps of the Dawn,
Whose blushing smile floods all the Orient;
And now bright Lucifer grows less and less,
Into the heaven's blue quiet deep-withdrawn.
Sunless and starless all, the desert sky
Arches above me, empty as this heart
For ages hath been empty of all joy,
Except to brood upon its silent hope,
As o'er its hope of day the sky doth now.
All night have I heard voices: deeper yet
The deep low breathing of the silence grew,
While all about, muffled in awe, there stood
Shadows, or forms, or both, clear-felt at heart,
But, when I turned to front them, far along
Only a shudder through the midnight ran,
And the dense stillness walled me closer round.
But still I heard them wander up and down
That solitude, and flappings of dusk wings
Did mingle with them, whether of those hags
Let slip upon me once from Hades deep,
Or of yet direr torments, if such be,
I could but guess; and then toward me came
A shape as of a woman: very pale

It was, and calm; its cold eyes did not move,
And mine moved not, but only stared on them.
Their fixëd awe went through my brain like ice;
A skeleton hand seemed clutching at my heart,
And a sharp chill, as if a dank night fog
Suddenly closed me in, was all I felt :
And then, methought, I heard a freezing sigh,
A long, deep, shivering sigh, as from blue lips
Stiffening in death, close to mine ear. I thought
Some doom was close upon me, and I looked
And saw the red moon through the heavy mist,
Just setting, and it seemed as it were falling,
Or reeling to its fall, so dim and dead
And palsy-struck it looked. Then all sounds merged
Into the rising surges of the pines,
Which, leagues below me, clothing the gaunt loins
Of ancient Caucasus with hairy strength,
Sent up a murmur in the morning wind,
Sad as the wail that from the populous earth
All day and night to high Olympus soars,
Fit incense to thy wicked throne, O Jove!

    Thy hated name is tossed once more in scorn
From off my lips, for I will tell thy doom.
And are these tears ? Nay, do not triumph, Jove!
They are wrung from me but by the agonies
Of prophecy, like those sparse drops which fall
From clouds in travail of the lightning, when
The great wave of the storm high-curled and black
Rolls steadily onward to its thunderous break.
Why art thou made a god of, thou poor type
Of anger, and revenge, and cunning force ?
    I

True Power was never born of brutish Strength,
Nor sweet Truth suckled at the shaggy dugs
Of that old she-wolf. Are thy thunderbolts,
That quell the darkness for a space, so strong
As the prevailing patience of meek Light,
Who, with the invincible tenderness of peace,
Wins it to be a portion of herself?
Why art thou made a god of, thou, who hast
The never-sleeping terror at thy heart,
That birthright of all tyrants, worse to bear
Than this thy ravening bird on which I smile?
Thou swear'st to free me, if I will unfold
What kind of doom it is whose omen flits
Across thy heart, as o'er a troop of doves
The fearful shadow of the kite. What need
To know that truth whose knowledge cannot save?
Evil its errand hath, as well as Good;
When thine is finished, thou art known no more:
There is a higher purity than thou,
And higher purity is greater strength;
Thy nature is thy doom, at which thy heart
Trembles behind the thick wall of thy might.
Let man but hope, and thou art straightway chilled
With thought of that drear silence and deep night
Which, like a dream, shall swallow thee and thine:
Let man but will, and thou art god no more,
More capable of ruin than the gold
And ivory that image thee on earth.
He who hurled down the monstrous Titan-brood
Blinded with lightnings, with rough thunders stunned,
Is weaker than a simple human thought.
My slender voice can shake thee, as the breeze,

That seems but apt to stir a maiden's hair,
Sways huge Oceanus from pole to pole ;
For I am still Prometheus, and foreknow
In my wise heart the end and doom of all.

Yes, I am still Prometheus, wiser grown
By years of solitude, — that holds apart
The past and future, giving the soul room
To search into itself, — and long commune
With this eternal silence ; — more a god,
In my long-suffering and strength to meet
With equal front the direst shafts of fate,
Than thou in thy faint-hearted despotism,
Girt with thy baby-toys of force and wrath.
Yes, I am that Prometheus who brought down
The light to man, which thou, in selfish fear,
Hadst to thyself usurped, — his by sole right,
For Man hath right to all save Tyranny, —
And which shall free him yet from thy frail throne.
Tyrants are but the spawn of Ignorance,
Begotten by the slaves they trample on,
Who, could they win a glimmer of the light,
And see that Tyranny is always weakness,
Or Fear with its own bosom ill at ease,
Would laugh away in scorn the sand-wove chain
Which their own blindness feigned for adamant.
Wrong ever builds on quicksands, but the Right
To the firm centre lays its moveless base.
The tyrant trembles, if the air but stir
The innocent ringlets of a child's free hair,
And crouches, when the thought of some great
        spirit,

With world-wide murmur, like a rising gale,
Over men's hearts, as over standing corn,
Rushes, and bends them to its own strong will.
So shall some thought of mine yet circle earth,
And puff away thy crumbling altars, Jove!

And, wouldst thou know of my supreme revenge,
Poor tyrant, even now dethroned in heart,
Realmless in soul, as tyrants ever are,
Listen! and tell me if this bitter peak,
This never-glutted vulture, and these chains
Shrink not before it; for it shall befit
A sorrow-taught, unconquered Titan-heart.
Men, when their death is on them, seem to stand
On a precipitous crag that overhangs
The abyss of doom, and in that depth to see,
As in a glass, the features dim and vast
Of things to come, the shadows, as it seems,
Of what have been. Death ever fronts the wise;
Not fearfully, but with clear promises
Of larger life, on whose broad vans upborne,
Their outlook widens, and they see beyond
The horizon of the Present and the Past,
Even to the very source and end of things.
Such am I now : immortal woe hath made
My heart a seer, and my soul a judge
Between the substance and the shadow of Truth.
The sure supremeness of the Beautiful,
By all the martyrdoms made doubly sure
Of such as I am, this is my revenge,
Which of my wrongs builds a triumphal arch,
Through which I see a sceptre and a throne.

The pipings of glad shepherds on the hills,
Tending the flocks no more to bleed for thee;
The songs of maidens pressing with white feet
The vintage on thine altars poured no more;
The murmurous bliss of lovers underneath
Dim grapevine bowers whose rosy bunches press
Not half so closely their warm cheeks, unpaled
By thoughts of thy brute lust; the hive-like hum
Of peaceful commonwealths, where sunburnt Toil
Reaps for itself the rich earth made its own
By its own labor, lightened with glad hymns
To an omnipotence which thy mad bolts
Would cope with as a spark with the vast sea, —
Even the spirit of free love and peace,
Duty's sure recompense through life and death, —
These are such harvests as all master-spirits
Reap, haply not on earth, but reap no less
Because the sheaves are bound by hands not theirs;
These are the bloodless daggers wherewithal
They stab fallen tyrants, this their high revenge:
For their best part of life on earth is when,
Long after death, prisoned and pent no more,
Their thoughts, their wild dreams even, have become
Part of the necessary air men breathe:
When, like the moon, herself behind a cloud,
They shed down light before us on life's sea,
That cheers us to steer onward still in hope.
Earth with her twining memories ivies o'er
Their holy sepulchres; the chainless sea,
In tempest or wide calm, repeats their thoughts;
The lightning and the thunder, all free things,

Have legends of them for the ears of men.
All other glories are as falling stars,
But universal Nature watches theirs :
Such strength is won by love of human kind.

Not that I feel that hunger after fame,
Which souls of a half-greatness are beset with ;
But that the memory of noble deeds
Cries shame upon the idle and the vile,
And keeps the heart of Man forever up
To the heroic level of old time.
To be forgot at first is little pain
To a heart conscious of such high intent
As must be deathless on the lips of men ;
But, having been a name, to sink and be
A something which the world can do without,
Which, having been or not, would never change
The lightest pulse of fate, — this is indeed
A cup of bitterness the worst to taste,
And this thy heart shall empty to the dregs.
Endless despair shall be thy Caucasus,
And memory thy vulture ; thou wilt find
Oblivion far lonelier than this peak.
Behold thy destiny ! Thou think'st it much
That I should brave thee, miserable god !
But I have braved a mightier than thou,
Even the sharp tempting of this soaring heart,
Which might have made me, scarcely less than thou,
A god among my brethren weak and blind,
Scarce less than thou, a pitiable thing
To be down-trodden into darkness soon.
But now I am above thee, for thou art

The bungling workmanship of fear, the block
That awes the swart Barbarian; but I
Am what myself have made, — a nature wise
With finding in itself the types of all,
With watching from the dim verge of the time
What things to be are visible in the gleams
Thrown forward on them from the luminous past,
Wise with the history of its own frail heart,
With reverence and with sorrow, and with love,
Broad as the world, for freedom and for man.

Thou and all strength shall crumble, except Love,
By whom, and for whose glory, ye shall cease:
And, when thou 'rt but a weary moaning heard
From out the pitiless gloom of Chaos, I
Shall be a power and a memory,
A name to fright all tyrants with, a light
Unsetting as the pole-star, a great voice
Heard in the breathless pauses of the fight
By truth and freedom ever waged with wrong,
Clear as a silver trumpet, to awake
Far echoes that from age to age live on
In kindred spirits, giving them a sense
Of boundless power from boundless suffering wrung:
And many a glazing eye shall smile to see
The memory of my triumph (for to meet
Wrong with endurance, and to overcome
The present with a heart that looks beyond,
Are triumph), like a prophet eagle, perch
Upon the sacred banner of the Right.
Evil springs up, and flowers, and bears no seed,
And feeds the green earth with its swift decay,

Leaving it richer for the growth of truth;
But Good, once put in action or in thought,
Like a strong oak, doth from its boughs shed down
The ripe germs of a forest. Thou, weak god,
Shalt fade and be forgotten! but this soul,
Fresh-living still in the serene abyss,
In every heaving shall partake, that grows
From heart to heart among the sons of men, —
As the ominous hum before the earthquake runs
Far through the Ægean from roused isle to isle, —
Foreboding wreck to palaces and shrines,
And mighty rents in many a cavernous error
That darkens the free light to man : — This heart,
Unscarred by thy grim vulture, as the truth
Grows but more lovely 'neath the beaks and claws
Of Harpies blind that fain would soil it, shall
In all the throbbing exultations share
That wait on freedom's triumphs, and in all
The glorious agonies of martyr-spirits,
Sharp lightning-throws to split the jagged clouds
That veil the future, showing them the end,
Pain's thorny crown for constancy and truth,
Girding the temples like a wreath of stars.
This is a thought, that, like the fabled laurel,
Makes my faith thunder-proof; and thy dread bolts
Fall on me like the silent flakes of snow
On the hoar brows of aged Caucasus :
But, oh, thought far more blissful, they can rend
This cloud of flesh, and make my soul a star!

Unleash thy crouching thunders now, O Jove!
Free this high heart, which, a poor captive long,

Doth knock to be let forth, this heart which still,
In its invincible manhood, overtops
Thy puny godship, as this mountain doth
The pines that moss its roots. Oh, even now,
While from my peak of suffering I look down,
Beholding with a far-spread gush of hope
The sunrise of that Beauty, in whose face,
Shone all around with love, no man shall look
But straightway like a god he be uplift
Unto the throne long empty for his sake,
And clearly oft foreshadowed in brave dreams
By his free inward nature, which nor thou,
Nor any anarch after thee, can bind
From working its great doom, — now, now set free
This essence, not to die, but to become
Part of that awful Presence which doth haunt
The palaces of tyrants, to scare off,
With its grim eyes and fearful whisperings
And hideous sense of utter loneliness,
All hope of safety, all desire of peace,
All but the loathed forefeeling of blank death, —
Part of that spirit which doth ever brood
In patient calm on the unpilfered nest
Of man's deep heart, till mighty thoughts grow fledged
To sail with darkening shadow o'er the world,
Filling with dread such souls as dare not trust
In the unfailing energy of Good,
Until they swoop, and their pale quarry make
Of some o'erbloated wrong, — that spirit which
Scatters great hopes in the seed-field of man,
Like acorns among grain, to grow and be
A roof for freedom in all coming time !

But no, this cannot be ; for ages yet,
In solitude unbroken, shall I hear
The angry Caspian to the Euxine shout,
And Euxine answer with a muffled roar,
On either side storming the giant walls
Of Caucasus with leagues of climbing foam
(Less, from my height, than flakes of downy snow),
That draw back baffled but to hurl again,
Snatched up in wrath and horrible turmoil,
Mountain on mountain, as the Titans erst,
My brethren, scaling the high seat of Jove,
Heaved Pelion upon Ossa's shoulders broad
In vain emprise. The moon will come and go
With her monotonous vicissitude ;
Once beautiful, when I was free to walk
Among my fellows, and to interchange
The influence benign of loving eyes,
But now by aged use grown wearisome ; —
False thought ! most false ! for how could I endure
These crawling centuries of lonely woe
Unshamed by weak complaining, but for thee,
Loneliest, save me, of all created things,
Mild-eyed Astarte, my best comforter,
With thy pale smile of sad benignity ?

Year after year will pass away and seem
To me, in mine eternal agony,
But as the shadows of dumb summer clouds,
Which I have watched so often darkening o'er
The vast Sarmatian plain, league-wide at first,
But, with still swiftness, lessening on and on
Till cloud and shadow meet and mingle where

The gray horizon fades into the sky,
Far, far to northward. Yes, for ages yet
Must I lie here upon my altar huge,
A sacrifice for man. Sorrow will be,
As it hath been, his portion; endless doom,
While the immortal with the mortal linked
Dreams of its wings and pines for what it dreams,
With upward yearn unceasing. Better so :
For wisdom is stern sorrow's patient child,
And empire over self, and all the deep
Strong charities that make men seem like gods ;
And love, that makes them be gods, from her
        breasts
Sucks in the milk that makes mankind one blood.
Good never comes unmixed, or so it seems,
Having two faces, as some images
Are carved, of foolish gods ; one face is ill ;
But one heart lies beneath, and that is good,
As are all hearts, when we explore their depths.
Therefore, great heart, bear up ! thou art but type
Of what all lofty spirits endure, that fain
Would win men back to strength and peace through
        love :
Each hath his lonely peak, and on each heart
Envy, or scorn, or hatred, tears lifelong
With vulture beak ; yet the high soul is left ;
And faith, which is but hope grown wise, and love
And patience which at last shall overcome.

THE SHEPHERD OF KING ADMETUS

THERE came a youth upon the earth,
　　Some thousand years ago,
Whose slender hands were nothing worth,
Whether to plough, or reap, or sow.

Upon an empty tortoise-shell
　　He stretched some chords, and drew
Music that made men's bosoms swell
Fearless, or brimmed their eyes with dew.

Then King Admetus, one who had
　　Pure taste by right divine,
Decreed his singing not too bad
To hear between the cups of wine:

And so, well pleased with being soothed
　　Into a sweet half-sleep,
Three times his kingly beard he smoothed,
And made him viceroy o'er his sheep.

His words were simple words enough,
　　And yet he used them so,
That what in other mouths was rough
In his seemed musical and low.

Men called him but a shiftless youth,
　　In whom no good they saw;

And yet, unwittingly, in truth,
They made his careless words their law.

They knew not how he learned at all,
   For idly, hour by hour,
He sat and watched the dead leaves fall,
Or mused upon a common flower.

It seemed the loveliness of things
   Did teach him all their use,
For, in mere weeds, and stones, and springs,
He found a healing power profuse.

Men granted that his speech was wise,
   But, when a glance they caught
Of his slim grace and woman's eyes,
They laughed, and called him good-for-naught.

Yet after he was dead and gone,
   And e'en his memory dim,
Earth seemed more sweet to live upon,
More full of love, because of him.

And day by day more holy grew
   Each spot where he had trod,
Till after-poets only knew
Their first-born brother as a god.

THE TOKEN

It is a mere wild rosebud,
    Quite sallow now, and dry,
Yet there's something wondrous in it,
    Some gleams of days gone by,
Dear sights and sounds that are to me
The very moons of memory,
And stir my heart's blood far below
Its short-lived waves of joy and woe.

Lips must fade and roses wither,
    All sweet times be o'er;
They only smile, and, murmuring " Thither ! "
    Stay with us no more:
And yet ofttimes a look or smile,
Forgotten in a kiss's while,
Years after from the dark will start,
And flash across the trembling heart.

Thou hast given me many roses,
    But never one, like this,
O'erfloods both sense and spirit
    With such a deep, wild bliss;
We must have instincts that glean up
Sparse drops of this life in the cup,
Whose taste shall give us all that we
Can prove of immortality.

Earth's stablest things are shadows,
   And, in the life to come,
Haply some chance-saved trifle
   May tell of this old home :
As now sometimes we seem to find,
In a dark crevice of the mind,
Some relic, which, long pondered o'er,
Hints faintly at a life before.

AN INCIDENT IN A RAILROAD CAR

HE spoke of Burns : men rude and rough
Pressed round to hear the praise of one
Whose heart was made of manly, simple stuff,
   As homespun as their own.

And, when he read, they forward leaned,
   Drinking, with thirsty hearts and ears,
His brook-like songs whom glory never weaned
   From humble smiles and tears.

Slowly there grew a tender awe,
   Sun-like, o'er faces brown and hard,
As if in him who read they felt and saw
   Some presence of the bard.

It was a sight for sin and wrong
   And slavish tyranny to see,
A sight to make our faith more pure and strong
   In high humanity.

I thought, these men will carry hence
Promptings their former life above,
And something of a finer reverence
    For beauty, truth, and love.

God scatters love on every side
Freely among his children all,
And always hearts are lying open wide,
    Wherein some grains may fall.

There is no wind but soweth seeds
Of a more true and open life,
Which burst, unlooked for, into high-souled deeds,
    With wayside beauty rife.

We find within these souls of ours
Some wild germs of a higher birth,
Which in the poet's tropic heart bear flowers
    Whose fragrance fills the earth.

Within the hearts of all men lie
These promises of wider bliss,
Which blossom into hopes that cannot die,
    In sunny hours like this.

All that hath been majestical
In life or death, since time began,
Is native in the simple heart of all,
    The angel heart of man.

And thus, among the untaught poor,
Great deeds and feelings find a home,

That cast in shadow all the golden lore
    Of classic Greece and Rome.

O mighty brother-soul of man,
    Where'er thou art, in low or high,
Thy skyey arches with exulting span
    O'er-roof infinity !

All thoughts that mould the age begin
    Deep down within the primitive soul,
And from the many slowly upward win
    To one who grasps the whole :

In his wide brain the feeling deep
    That struggled on the many's tongue
Swells to a tide of thought, whose surges leap
    O'er the weak thrones of wrong.

All thought begins in feeling, — wide
    In the great mass its base is hid,
And, narrowing up to thought, stands glorified,
    A moveless pyramid.

Nor is he far astray, who deems
    That every hope, which rises and grows broad
In the world's heart, by ordered impulse streams
    From the great heart of God.

God wills, man hopes : in common souls
    Hope is but vague and undefined,
Till from the poet's tongue the message rolls
    A blessing to his kind.

I

Never did Poesy appear
So full of heaven to me, as when
I saw how it would pierce through pride and fear
    To the lives of coarsest men.

It may be glorious to write
Thoughts that shall glad the two or three
High souls, like those far stars that come in sight
    Once in a century ; —

But better far it is to speak
One simple word, which now and then
Shall waken their free nature in the weak
    And friendless sons of men ;

To write some earnest verse or line,
Which, seeking not the praise of art,
Shall make a clearer faith and manhood shine
    In the untutored heart.

He who doth this, in verse or prose,
May be forgotten in his day,
But surely shall be crowned at last with those
    Who live and speak for aye.

RHŒCUS

GOD sends his teachers unto every age,
To every clime, and every race of men,
With revelations fitted to their growth
And shape of mind, nor gives the realm of Truth

Into the selfish rule of one sole race:
Therefore each form of worship that hath swayed
The life of man, and given it to grasp
The master-key of knowledge, reverence,
Infolds some germs of goodness and of right;
Else never had the eager soul, which loathes
The slothful down of pampered ignorance,
Found in it even a moment's fitful rest.

There is an instinct in the human heart
Which makes that all the fables it hath coined,
To justify the reign of its belief
And strengthen it by beauty's right divine,
Veil in their inner cells a mystic gift,
Which, like the hazel twig, in faithful hands,
Points surely to the hidden springs of truth.
For, as in Nature naught is made in vain,
But all things have within their hull of use
A wisdom and a meaning which may speak
Of spiritual secrets to the ear
Of spirit; so, in whatsoe'er the heart
Hath fashioned for a solace to itself,
To make its inspirations suit its creed,
And from the niggard hands of falsehood wring
Its needful food of truth, there ever is
A sympathy with Nature, which reveals,
Not less than her own works, pure gleams of light
And earnest parables of inward lore.
Hear now this fairy legend of old Greece,
As full of gracious youth, and beauty still
As the immortal freshness of that grace
Carved for all ages on some Attic frieze.

A youth named Rhœcus, wandering in the wood,
Saw an old oak just trembling to its fall,
And, feeling pity of so fair a tree,
He propped its gray trunk with admiring care,
And with a thoughtless footstep loitered on.
But, as he turned, he heard a voice behind
That murmured " Rhœcus! " 'T was as if the
        leaves,
Stirred by a passing breath, had murmured it,
And, while he paused bewildered, yet again
It murmured " Rhœcus! " softer than a breeze.
He started and beheld with dizzy eyes
What seemed the substance of a happy dream
Stand there before him, spreading a warm glow
Within the green glooms of the shadowy oak.
It seemed a woman's shape, yet far too fair
To be a woman, and with eyes too meek
For any that were wont to mate with gods.
All naked like a goddess stood she there,
And like a goddess all too beautiful
To feel the guilt-born earthliness of shame.
" Rhœcus, I am the Dryad of this tree,"
Thus she began, dropping her low-toned words
Serene, and full, and clear, as drops of dew,
" And with it I am doomed to live and die ;
The rain and sunshine are my caterers,
Nor have I other bliss than simple life ;
Now ask me what thou wilt, that I can give,
And with a thankful joy it shall be thine."

Then Rhœcus, with a flutter at the heart,
Yet, by the prompting of such beauty, bold,

Answered : " What is there that can satisfy
The endless craving of the soul but love ?
Give me thy love, or but the hope of that
Which must be evermore my nature's goal."
After a little pause she said again,
But with a glimpse of sadness in her tone,
" I give it, Rhœcus, though a perilous gift ;
An hour before the sunset meet me here."
And straightway there was nothing he could see
But the green glooms beneath the shadowy oak,
And not a sound came to his straining ears
But the low trickling rustle of the leaves,
And far away upon an emerald slope
The falter of an idle shepherd's pipe.

Now, in those days of simpleness and faith,
Men did not think that happy things were dreams
Because they overstepped the narrow bourn
Of likelihood, but reverently deemed
Nothing too wondrous or too beautiful
To be the guerdon of a daring heart.
So Rhœcus made no doubt that he was blest,
And all along unto the city's gate
Earth seemed to spring beneath him as he walked,
The clear, broad sky looked bluer than its wont,
And he could scarce believe he had not wings,
Such sunshine seemed to glitter through his veins
Instead of blood, so light he felt and strange.

Young Rhœcus had a faithful heart enough,
But one that in the present dwelt too much,
And, taking with blithe welcome whatsoe'er

Chance gave of joy, was wholly bound in that,
Like the contented peasant of a vale,
Deemed it the world, and never looked beyond.
So, haply meeting in the afternoon
Some comrades who were playing at the dice,
He joined them, and forgot all else beside.

　　The dice were rattling at the merriest,
And Rhœcus, who had met but sorry luck,
Just laughed in triumph at a happy throw,
When through the room there hummed a yellow bee
That buzzed about his ear with down-dropped legs
As if to light. And Rhœcus laughed and said,
Feeling how red and flushed he was with loss,
" By Venus ! does he take me for a rose ? "
And brushed him off with rough, impatient hand.
But still the bee came back, and thrice again
Rhœcus did beat him off with growing wrath.
Then through the window flew the wounded bee,
And Rhœcus, tracking him with angry eyes,
Saw a sharp mountain-peak of Thessaly
Against the red disk of the setting sun, —
And instantly the blood sank from his heart,
As if its very walls had caved away.
Without a word he turned, and, rushing forth,
Ran madly through the city and the gate,
And o'er the plain, which now the wood's long shade,
By the low sun thrown forward broad and dim,
Darkened well-nigh unto the city's wall.

　　Quite spent and out of breath he reached the tree,
And, listening fearfully, he heard once more

The low voice murmur " Rhœcus ! " close at hand :
Whereat he looked around him, but could see
Naught but the deepening glooms beneath the oak.
Then sighed the voice, " O Rhœcus ! nevermore
Shalt thou behold me or by day or night,
Me, who would fain have blessed thee with a love
More ripe and bounteous than ever yet
Filled up with nectar any mortal heart :
But thou didst scorn my humble messenger,
And sent'st him back to me with bruisëd wings.
We spirits only show to gentle eyes,
We ever ask an undivided love,
And he who scorns the least of Nature's works
Is thenceforth exiled and shut out from all.
Farewell ! for thou canst never see me more."

Then Rhœcus beat his breast, and groaned aloud,
And cried, " Be pitiful ! forgive me yet
This once, and I shall never need it more ! "
" Alas ! " the voice returned, " 't is thou art blind,
Not I unmerciful ; I can forgive,
But have no skill to heal thy spirit's eyes ;
Only the soul hath power o'er itself."
With that again there murmured " Nevermore ! "
And Rhœcus after heard no other sound,
Except the rattling of the oak's crisp leaves,
Like the long surf upon a distant shore,
Raking the sea-worn pebbles up and down.
The night had gathered round him : o'er the plain
The city sparkled with its thousand lights,
And sounds of revel fell upon his ear
Harshly and like a curse ; above, the sky,

With all its bright sublimity of stars,
Deepened, and on his forehead smote the breeze:
Beauty was all around him and delight,
But from that eve he was alone on earth.

THE FALCON

I know a falcon swift and peerless
  . As e'er was cradled in the pine;
No bird had ever eye so fearless,
    Or wing so strong as this of mine.

The winds not better love to pilot
    A cloud with molten gold o'errun,
Than him, a little burning islet,
    A star above the coming sun.

For with a lark's heart he doth tower,
    By a glorious upward instinct drawn;
No bee nestles deeper in the flower
    Than he in the bursting rose of dawn.

No harmless dove, no bird that singeth,
    Shudders to see him overhead;
The rush of his fierce swooping bringeth
    To innocent hearts no thrill of dread.

Let fraud and wrong and baseness shiver,
    For still between them and the sky
The falcon Truth hangs poised forever
    And marks them with his vengeful eye.

TRIAL

I

WHETHER the idle prisoner through his grate
Watches the waving of the grass-tuft small,
Which, having colonized its rift i' th' wall,
Accepts God's dole of good or evil fate,
And from the sky's just helmet draws its lot
Daily of shower or sunshine, cold or hot; —
Whether the closer captive of a creed,
· Cooped up from birth to grind out endless chaff,
Sees through his treadmill-bars the noonday laugh,
And feels in vain his crumpled pinions breed; —
Whether the Georgian slave look up and mark,
With bellying sails puffed full, the tall cloud-bark
Sink northward slowly, — thou alone seem'st good,
Fair only thou, O Freedom, whose desire
Can light in muddiest souls quick seeds of fire,
And strain life's chords to the old heroic mood.

II

Yet are there other gifts more fair than thine,
Nor can I count him happiest who has never
Been forced with his own hand his chains to sever,
And for himself find out the way divine;
He never knew the aspirer's glorious pains,
He never earned the struggle's priceless gains.
Oh, block by block, with sore and sharp endeavor,

Lifelong we build these human natures up
Into a temple fit for Freedom's shrine,
And Trial ever consecrates the cup
Wherefrom we pour her sacrificial wine.

A GLANCE BEHIND THE CURTAIN

WE see but half the causes of our deeds,
Seeking them wholly in the outer life,
And heedless of the encircling spirit-world,
Which, though unseen, is felt, and sows in us
All germs of pure and world-wide purposes.
From one stage of our being to the next
We pass unconscious o'er a slender bridge,
The momentary work of unseen hands,
Which crumbles down behind us ; looking back,
We see the other shore, the gulf between,
And, marvelling how we won to where we stand,
Content ourselves to call the builder Chance.
We trace the wisdom to the apple's fall,
Not to the birth-throes of a mighty Truth
Which, for long ages in blank Chaos dumb,
Yet yearned to be incarnate, and had found
At last a spirit meet to be the womb
From which it might be born to bless mankind, —
Not to the soul of Newton, ripe with all
The hoarded thoughtfulness of earnest years,
And waiting but one ray of sunlight more
To blossom fully.

But whence came that ray?
We call our sorrows Destiny, but ought
Rather to name our high successes so.
Only the instincts of great souls are Fate,
And have predestined sway: all other things,
Except by leave of us, could never be.
For Destiny is but the breath of God
Still moving in us, the last fragment left
Of our unfallen nature, waking oft
Within our thought, to beckon us beyond
The narrow circle of the seen and known,
And always tending to a noble end,
As all things must that overrule the soul,
And for a space unseat the helmsman, Will.
The fate of England and of freedom once
Seemed wavering in the heart of one plain man:
One step of his, and the great dial-hand,
That marks the destined progress of the world
In the eternal round from wisdom on
To higher wisdom, had been made to pause
A hundred years. That step he did not take, —
He knew not why, nor we, but only God, —
And lived to make his simple oaken chair
More terrible and soberly august,
More full of majesty than any throne,
Before or after, of a British king.

Upon the pier stood two stern-visaged men,
Looking to where a little craft lay moored,
Swayed by the lazy current of the Thames,
Which weltered by in muddy listlessness.
Grave men they were, and battlings of fierce thought

Had trampled out all softness from their brows,
And ploughed rough furrows there before their time,
For other crop than such as homebred Peace
Sows broadcast in the willing soil of Youth.
Care, not of self, but for the common weal,
Had robbed their eyes of youth, and left instead
A look of patient power and iron will,
And something fiercer, too, that gave broad hint
Of the plain weapons girded at their sides.
The younger had an aspect of command, —
Not such as trickles down, a slender stream,
In the shrunk channel of a great descent,
But such as lies entowered in heart and head,
And an arm prompt to do the 'hests of both.
His was a brow where gold were out of place,
And yet it seemed right worthy of a crown
(Though he despised such), were it only made
Of iron, or some serviceable stuff
That would have matched his brownly rugged face.
The elder, although such he hardly seemed
(Care makes so little of some five short years),
Had a clear, honest face, whose rough-hewn strength
Was mildened by the scholar's wiser heart
To sober courage, such as best befits
The unsullied temper of a well-taught mind,
Yet so remained that one could plainly guess
The hushed volcano smouldering underneath.
He spoke: the other, hearing, kept his gaze
Still fixed, as on some problem in the sky.

    " O CROMWELL, we are fallen on evil times!
There was a day when England had wide room

For honest men as well as foolish kings :
But now the uneasy stomach of the time
Turns squeamish at them both. Therefore let us
Seek out that savage clime, where men as yet
Are free : there sleeps the vessel on the tide,
Her languid canvas drooping for the wind ;
Give us but that, and what need we to fear
This Order of the Council ? The free waves
Will not say No to please a wayward king,
Nor will the winds turn traitors at his beck :
All things are fitly cared for, and the Lord
Will watch as kindly o'er the exodus
Of us his servants now, as in old time.
We have no cloud or fire, and haply we
May not pass dry-shod through the ocean-stream ;
But, saved or lost, all things are in His hand."
So spake he, and meantime the other stood
With wide gray eyes still reading the blank air,
As if upon the sky's blue wall he saw
Some mystic sentence, written by a hand,
Such as of old made pale the Assyrian king,
Girt with his satraps in the blazing feast.

" HAMPDEN ! a moment since, my purpose was
To fly with thee, — for I will call it flight,
Nor flatter it with any smoother name, —
But something in me bids me not to go ;
And I am one, thou knowest, who, unmoved
By what the weak deem omens, yet give heed
And reverence due to whatsoe'er my soul
Whispers of warning to the inner ear.
Moreover, as I know that God brings round

His purposes in ways undreamed by us,
And makes the wicked but His instruments
To hasten their own swift and sudden fall,
I see the beauty of His providence
In the King's order: blind, he will not let
His doom part from him, but must bid it stay
As 't were a cricket, whose enlivening chirp
He loved to hear beneath his very hearth.
Why should we fly? Nay, why not rather stay
And rear again our Zion's crumbled walls,
Not, as of old the walls of Thebes were built,
By minstrel twanging, but, if need should be,
With the more potent music of our swords?
Think'st thou that score of men beyond the sea
Claim more God's care than all of England here?
No: when He moves His arm, it is to aid
Whole peoples, heedless if a few be crushed,
As some are ever, when the destiny
Of man takes one stride onward nearer home.
Believe me, 't is the mass of men He loves;
And, where there is most sorrow and most want,
Where the high heart of man is trodden down
The most, 't is not because He hides His face
From them in wrath, as purblind teachers prate:
Not so: there most is He, for there is He
Most needed. Men who seek for Fate abroad
Are not so near His heart as they who dare
Frankly to face her where she faces them,
On their own threshold, where their souls are strong
To grapple with and throw her; as I once,
Being yet a boy, did cast this puny king,
Who now has grown so dotard as to deem

That he can wrestle with an angry realm,
And throw the brawned Antæus of men's rights.
No, Hampden! they have halfway conquered Fate
Who go halfway to meet her, — as will I.
Freedom hath yet a work for me to do;
So speaks that inward voice which never yet
Spake falsely, when it urged the spirit on
To noble emprise for country and mankind.
And, for success, I ask no more than this, —
To bear unflinching witness to the truth.
All true whole men succeed; for what is worth
Success's name, unless it be the thought,
The inward surety, to have carried out
A noble purpose to a noble end,
Although it be the gallows or the block?
'T is only Falsehood that doth ever need
These outward shows of gain to bolster her.
Be it we prove the weaker with our swords;
Truth only needs to be for once spoke out,
And there 's such music in her, such strange rhythm,
As makes men's memories her joyous slaves,
And clings around the soul, as the sky clings
Round the mute earth, forever beautiful,
And, if o'erclouded, only to burst forth
More all-embracingly divine and clear:
Get but the truth once uttered, and 't is like
A star new-born, that drops into its place,
And which, once circling in its placid round,
Not all the tumult of the earth can shake.

  " What should we do in that small colony
Of pinched fanatics, who would rather choose

Freedom to clip an inch more from their hair,
Than the great chance of setting England free?
Not there, amid the stormy wilderness,
Should we learn wisdom; or if learned, what room
To put it into act, — else worse than naught?
We learn our souls more, tossing for an hour
Upon this huge and ever-vexëd sea
Of human thought, where kingdoms go to wreck
Like fragile bubbles yonder in the stream,
Than in a cycle of New England sloth,
Broke only by a petty Indian war,
Or quarrel for a letter more or less
In some hard word, which, spelt in either way,
Not their most learnëd clerks can understand.
New times demand new measures and new men;
The world advances, and in time outgrows
The laws that in our fathers' day were best;
And, doubtless, after us, some purer scheme
Will be shaped out by wiser men than we,
Made wiser by the steady growth of truth.
We cannot hale Utopia on by force;
But better, almost, be at work in sin,
Than in a brute inaction browse and sleep.
No man is born into the world whose work
Is not born with him; there is always work,
And tools to work withal, for those who will;
And blessëd are the horny hands of toil!
The busy world shoves angrily aside
The man who stands with arms akimbo set,
Until occasion tells him what to do;
And he who waits to have his task marked out
Shall die and leave his errand unfulfilled.

Our time is one that calls for earnest deeds :
Reason and Government, like two broad seas,
Yearn for each other with outstretchëd arms
Across this narrow isthmus of the throne,
And roll their white surf higher every day.
One age moves onward, and the next builds up
Cities and gorgeous palaces, where stood
The rude log huts of those who tamed the wild,
Rearing from out the forests they had felled
The goodly framework of a fairer state ;
The builder's trowel and the settler's axe
Are seldom wielded by the selfsame hand ;
Ours is the harder task, yet not the less
Shall we receive the blessing for our toil
From the choice spirits of the aftertime.
My soul is not a palace of the past,
Where outworn creeds, like Rome's gray senate, quake,
Hearing afar the Vandal's trumpet hoarse,
That shakes old systems with a thunder-fit.
The time is ripe, and rotten-ripe, for change ;
Then let it come : I have no dread of what
Is called for by the instinct of mankind ;
Nor think I that God's world will fall apart
Because we tear a parchment more or less.
Truth is eternal, but her effluence,
With endless change, is fitted to the hour ;
Her mirror is turned forward to reflect
The promise of the future, not the past.
He who would win the name of truly great
Must understand his own age and the next,
And make the present ready to fulfil
Its prophecy, and with the future merge

I

Gently and peacefully, as wave with wave.
The future works out great men's purposes;
The present is enough for common souls,
Who, never looking forward, are indeed
Mere clay, wherein the footprints of their age
Are petrified forever : better those
Who lead the blind old giant by the hand
From out the pathless desert where he gropes,
And set him onward in his darksome way.
I do not fear to follow out the truth,
Albeit along the precipice's edge.
Let us speak plain: there is more force in names
Than most men dream of; and a lie may keep
Its throne a whole age longer, if it skulk
Behind the shield of some fair-seeming name.
Let us call tyrants *tyrants*, and maintain
That only freedom comes by grace of God,
And all that comes not by His grace must fall;
For men in earnest have no time to waste
In patching fig-leaves for the naked truth.

"I will have one more grapple with the man
Charles Stuart : whom the boy o'ercame,
The man stands not in awe of. I, perchance,
Am one raised up by the Almighty arm
To witness some great truth to all the world.
Souls destined to o'erleap the vulgar lot,
And mould the world unto the scheme of God,
Have a fore-consciousness of their high doom,
As men are known to shiver at the heart
When the cold shadow of some coming ill
Creeps slowly o'er their spirits unawares.

Hath Good less power of prophecy than Ill?
How else could men whom God hath called to sway
Earth's rudder, and to steer the bark of Truth,
Beating against the tempest tow'rd her port,
Bear all the mean and buzzing grievances,
The petty martyrdoms, wherewith Sin strives
To weary out the tethered hope of Faith?
The sneers, the unrecognizing look of friends,
Who worship the dead corpse of old king Custom,
Where it doth lie in state within the Church,
Striving to cover up the mighty ocean
With a man's palm, and making even the truth
Lie for them, holding up the glass reversed,
To make the hope of man seem farther off?
My God! when I read o'er the bitter lives
Of men whose eager hearts were quite too great
To beat beneath the cramped mode of the day,
And see them mocked at by the world they love,
Haggling with prejudice for pennyworths
Of that reform which their hard toil will make
The common birthright of the age to come,—
When I see this, spite of my faith in God,
I marvel how their hearts bear up so long;
Nor could they but for this same prophecy,
This inward feeling of the glorious end.

" Deem me not fond; but in my warmer youth,
Ere my heart's bloom was soiled and brushed away,
I had great dreams of mighty things to come;
Of conquest, whether by the sword or pen
I knew not; but some conquest I would have,
Or else swift death: now wiser grown in years,

I find youth's dreams are but the flutterings
Of those strong wings whereon the soul shall soar
In aftertime to win a starry throne;
And so I cherish them, for they were lots,
Which I, a boy, cast in the helm of Fate.
Now will I draw them, since a man's right hand,
A right hand guided by an earnest soul,
With a true instinct, takes the golden prize
From out a thousand blanks. What men call luck
Is the prerogative of valiant souls,
The fealty life pays its rightful kings.
The helm is shaking now, and I will stay
To pluck my lot forth; it were sin to flee!"

So they two turned together; one to die,
Fighting for freedom on the bloody field;
The other, far more happy, to become
A name earth wears forever next her heart;
One of the few that have a right to rank
With the true Makers: for his spirit wrought
Order from Chaos; proved that right divine
Dwelt only in the excellence of truth;
And far within old Darkness' hostile lines
Advanced and pitched the shining tents of Light.
Nor shall the grateful Muse forget to tell,
That — not the least among his many claims
To deathless honor — he was MILTON'S friend,
A man not second among those who lived
To show us that the poet's lyre demands
An arm of tougher sinew than the sword.

A CHIPPEWA LEGEND [1]

ἀλγεινὰ μέν μοι καὶ λέγειν ἐστὶν τάδε,
ἄλγος δὲ σιγᾶν.
ÆSCHYLUS, *Prom. Vinct.* 197, 198.

THE old Chief, feeling now well-nigh his end,
Called his two eldest children to his side,
And gave them, in few words, his parting charge !
" My son and daughter, me ye see no more ;
The happy hunting-grounds await me, green
With change of spring and summer through the year :
But, for remembrance, after I am gone,
Be kind to little Sheemah for my sake :
Weakling he is and young, and knows not yet
To set the trap, or draw the seasoned bow ;
Therefore of both your loves he hath more need,
And he, who needeth love, to love hath right ;
It is not like our furs and stores of corn,
Whereto we claim sole title by our toil,
But the Great Spirit plants it in our hearts,
And waters it, and gives it sun, to be
The common stock and heritage of all :
Therefore be kind to Sheemah, that yourselves
May not be left deserted in your need."

Alone, beside a lake, their wigwam stood,
Far from the other dwellings of their tribe ;

[1] For the leading incidents in this tale I am indebted to the very valuable *Algic Researches* of Henry R. Schoolcraft, Esq.

And, after many moons, the loneliness
Wearied the elder brother, and he said,
" Why should I dwell here far from men, shut out
From the free, natural joys that fit my age?
Lo, I am tall and strong, well skilled to hunt,
Patient of toil and hunger, and not yet
Have seen the danger which I dared not look
Full in the face; what hinders me to be
A mighty Brave and Chief among my kin?"
So, taking up his arrows and his bow,
As if to hunt, he journeyed swiftly on,
Until he gained the wigwams of his tribe,
Where, choosing out a bride, he soon forgot,
In all the fret and bustle of new life,
The little Sheemah and his father's charge.

Now when the sister found her brother gone,
And that, for many days he came not back,
She wept for Sheemah more than for herself;
For Love bides longest in a woman's heart,
And flutters many times before he flies,
And then doth perch so nearly, that a word
May lure him back to his accustomed nest;
And Duty lingers even when Love is gone,
Oft looking out in hope of his return;
And, after Duty hath been driven forth,
Then Selfishness creeps in the last of all,
Warming her lean hands at the lonely hearth,
And crouching o'er the embers, to shut out
Whatever paltry warmth and light are left,
With avaricious greed, from all beside.
So, for long months, the sister hunted wide,

And cared for little Sheemah tenderly;
But, daily more and more, the loneliness
Grew wearisome, and to herself she sighed,
" Am I not fair? at least the glassy pool,
That hath no cause to flatter, tells me so;
But, oh, how flat and meaningless the tale,
Unless it tremble on a lover's tongue!
Beauty hath no true glass, except it be
In the sweet privacy of loving eyes."
Thus deemed she idly, and forgot the lore
Which she had learned of Nature and the woods,
That beauty's chief reward is to itself,
And that Love's mirror holds no image long
Save of the inward fairness, blurred and lost
Unless kept clear and white by Duty's care.
So she went forth and sought the haunts of men,
And, being wedded, in her household cares,
Soon, like the elder brother, quite forgot
The little Sheemah and her father's charge.

But Sheemah, left alone within the lodge,
Waited and waited, with a shrinking heart,
Thinking each rustle was his sister's step,
Till hope grew less and less, and then went out,
And every sound was changed from hope to fear.
Few sounds there were : — the dropping of a nut,
The squirrel's chirrup, and the jay's harsh scream,
Autumn's sad remnants of blithe Summer's cheer,
Heard at long intervals, seemed but to make
The dreadful void of silence silenter.
Soon what small store his sister left was gone,
And, through the Autumn, he made shift to live

On roots and berries, gathered in much fear
Of wolves, whose ghastly howl he heard ofttimes,
Hollow and hungry, at the dead of night.
But Winter came at last, and, when the snow,
Thick-heaped for gleaming leagues o'er hill and
      plain,
Spread its unbroken silence over all,
Made bold by hunger, he was fain to glean
(More sick at heart than Ruth, and all alone)
After the harvest of the merciless wolf,
Grim Boaz, who, sharp-ribbed and gaunt, yet feared
A thing more wild and starving than himself;
Till, by degrees, the wolf and he grew friends,
And shared together all the Winter through.

Late in the Spring, when all the ice was gone,
The elder brother, fishing in the lake,
Upon whose edge his father's wigwam stood,
Heard a low moaning noise upon the shore:
Half like a child it seemed, half like a wolf,
And straightway there was something in his heart
That said, " It is thy brother Sheemah's voice."
So, paddling swiftly to the bank, he saw,
Within a little thicket close at hand,
A child that seemed fast changing to a wolf,
From the neck downward, gray with shaggy hair,
That still crept on and upward as he looked.
The face was turned away, but well he knew
That it was Sheemah's, even his brother's face.
Then with his trembling hands he hid his eyes,
And bowed his head, so that he might not see
The first look of his brother's eyes, and cried,

" O Sheemah! O my brother, speak to me !
  Dost thou not know me, that I am thy brother?
  Come to me, little Sheemah, thou shalt dwell
  With me henceforth, and know no care or want!"
  Sheemah was silent for a space, as if
  'T were hard to summon up a human voice,
  And, when he spake, the voice was as a wolf's :
" I know thee not, nor art thou what thou say'st;
  I have none other brethren than the wolves,
  And, till thy heart be changed from what it is,
  Thou art not worthy to be called their kin."
  Then groaned the other, with a choking tongue,
" Alas! my heart is changed right bitterly;
  'T is shrunk and parched within me even now!"
  And, looking upward fearfully, he saw
  Only a wolf that shrank away and ran,
  Ugly and fierce, to hide among the woods.

STANZAS ON FREEDOM

Men! whose boast it is that ye
Come of fathers brave and free,
If there breathe on earth a slave,
Are ye truly free and brave?
If ye do not feel the chain,
When it works a brother's pain,
Are ye not base slaves indeed,
Slaves unworthy to be freed?

Women! who shall one day bear
Sons to breathe New England air,

If ye hear, without a blush,
Deeds to make the roused blood rush
Like red lava through your veins,
For your sisters now in chains, —
Answer! are ye fit to be
Mothers of the brave and free?

Is true Freedom but to break
Fetters for our own dear sake,
And, with leathern hearts, forget
That we owe mankind a debt?
No! true Freedom is to share
All the chains our brothers wear,
And, with heart and hand, to be
Earnest to make others free!

They are slaves who fear to speak
For the fallen and the weak;
They are slaves who will not choose
Hatred, scoffing, and abuse,
Rather than in silence shrink
From the truth they needs must think;
They are slaves who dare not be
In the right with two or three.

COLUMBUS

THE cordage creaks and rattles in the wind,
With whims of sudden hush; the reeling sea
Now thumps like solid rock beneath the stern,
Now leaps with clumsy wrath, strikes short, and,
    falling

Crumbled to whispery foam, slips rustling down
The broad backs of the waves, which jostle and crowd
To fling themselves upon that unknown shore,
Their used familiar since the dawn of time,
Whither this foredoomed life is guided on
To sway on triumph's hushed, aspiring poise
One glittering moment, then to break fulfilled.

How lonely is the sea's perpetual swing,
The melancholy wash of endless waves,
The sigh of some grim monster undescried,
Fear-painted on the canvas of the dark,
Shifting on his uneasy pillow of brine!
Yet night brings more companions than the day
To this drear waste; new constellations burn,
And fairer stars, with whose calm height my soul
Finds nearer sympathy than with my herd
Of earthen souls, whose vision's scanty ring
Makes me its prisoner to beat my wings
Against the cold bars of their unbelief,
Knowing in vain my own free heaven beyond.
O God! this world, so crammed with eager life,
That comes and goes and wanders back to silence
Like the idle wind, which yet man's shaping mind
Can make his drudge to swell the longing sails
Of highest endeavor, — this mad, unthrift world,
Which, every hour, throws life enough away
To make her deserts kind and hospitable,
Lets her great destinies be waved aside
By smooth, lip-reverent, formal infidels,
Who weigh the God they not believe with gold,
And find no spot in Judas, save that he,

Driving a duller bargain than he ought,
Saddled his guild with too cheap precedent.
O Faith! if thou art strong, thine opposite
Is mighty also, and the dull fool's sneer
Hath ofttimes shot chill palsy through the arm
Just lifted to achieve its crowning deed,
And made the firm-based heart, that would have
    quailed
The rack or fagot, shudder like a leaf
Wrinkled with frost, and loose upon its stem.
The wicked and the weak, by some dark law,
Have a strange power to shut and rivet down
Their own horizon round us, to unwing
Our heaven-aspiring visions, and to blur
With surly clouds the Future's gleaming peaks,
Far seen across the brine of thankless years.
If the chosen soul could never be alone
In deep mid-silence, open-doored to God,
No greatness ever had been dreamed or done;
Among dull hearts a prophet never grew;
The nurse of full-grown souls is solitude.

The old world is effete; there man with man
Jostles, and, in the brawl for means to live,
Life is trod underfoot, — Life, the one block
Of marble that's vouchsafed wherefrom to carve
Our great thoughts, white and godlike, to shine down
The future, Life, the irredeemable block,
Which one o'er-hasty chisel-dint oft mars,
Scanting our room to cut the features out
Of our full hope, so forcing us to crown
With a mean head the perfect limbs, or leave

The god's face glowing o'er a satyr's trunk,
Failure's brief epitaph.

                     Yes, Europe's world
Reels on to judgment; there the common need,
Losing God's sacred use, to be a bond
'Twixt Me and Thee, sets each one scowlingly
O'er his own selfish hoard at bay; no state,
Knit strongly with eternal fibres up
Of all men's separate and united weals,
Self-poised and sole as stars, yet one as light,
Holds up a shape of large Humanity
To which by natural instinct every man
Pays loyalty exulting, by which all
Mould their own lives, and feel their pulses filled
With the red, fiery blood of the general life,
Making them mighty in peace, as now in war
They are, even in the flush of victory, weak,
Conquering that manhood which should them subdue.
And what gift bring I to this untried world?
Shall the same tragedy be played anew,
And the same lurid curtain drop at last
On one dread desolation, one fierce crash
Of that recoil which on its makers God
Lets Ignorance and Sin and Hunger make,
Early or late? Or shall that commonwealth
Whose potent unity and concentric force
Can draw these scattered joints and parts of men
Into a whole ideal man once more,
Which sucks not from its limbs the life away,
But sends it flood-tide and creates itself
Over again in every citizen,

Be there built up ? For me, I have no choice;
I might turn back to other destinies,
For one sincere key opes all Fortune's doors;
But whoso answers not God's earliest call
Forfeits or dulls that faculty supreme
Of lying open to his genius
Which makes the wise heart certain of its ends.

Here am I; for what end God knows, not I;
Westward still points the inexorable soul:
Here am I, with no friend but the sad sea,
The beating heart of this great enterprise,
Which, without me, would stiffen in swift death;
This have I mused on, since mine eye could first
Among the stars distinguish and with joy
Rest on that God-fed Pharos of the north,
On some blue promontory of heaven lighted
That juts far out into the upper sea;
To this one hope my heart hath clung for years,
As would a foundling to the talisman
Hung round his neck by hands he knew not whose;
A poor, vile thing and dross to all beside,
Yet he therein can feel a virtue left
By the sad pressure of a mother's hand,
And unto him it still is tremulous
With palpitating haste and wet with tears,
The key to him of hope and humanness,
The coarse shell of life's pearl, Expectancy.
This hope hath been to me for love and fame,
Hath made me wholly lonely on the earth,
Building me up as in a thick-ribbed tower,
Wherewith enwalled my watching spirit burned,

Conquering its little island from the Dark,
Sole as a scholar's lamp, and heard men's steps,
In the far hurry of the outward world,
Pass dimly forth and back, sounds heard in dream.
As Ganymede by the eagle was snatched up
From the gross sod to be Jove's cup-bearer,
So was I lifted by my great design:
And who hath trod Olympus, from his eye
Fades not that broader outlook of the gods;
His life's low valleys overbrow earth's clouds,
And that Olympian spectre of the past
Looms towering up in sovereign memory,
Beckoning his soul from meaner heights of doom.
Had but the shadow of the Thunderer's bird,
Flashing athwart my spirit, made of me
A swift-betraying vision's Ganymede,
Yet to have greatly dreamed precludes low ends;
Great days have ever such a morning-red,
On such a base great futures are built up,
And aspiration, though not put in act,
Comes back to ask its plighted troth again,
Still watches round its grave the unlaid ghost
Of a dead virtue, and makes other hopes,
Save that implacable one, seem thin and bleak
As shadows of bare trees upon the snow,
Bound freezing there by the unpitying moon.

While other youths perplexed their mandolins,
Praying that Thetis would her fingers twine
In the loose glories of her lover's hair,
And wile another kiss to keep back day,
I, stretched beneath the many-centuried shade

Of some writhed oak, the wood's Laocoön,
Did of my hope a dryad mistress make,
Whom I would woo to meet me privily,
Or underneath the stars, or when the moon
Flecked all the forest floor with scattered pearls.
O days whose memory tames to fawning down
The surly fell of Ocean's bristled neck!

I know not when this hope enthralled me first,
But from my boyhood up I loved to hear
The tall pine-forests of the Apennine
Murmur their hoary legends of the sea,
Which hearing, I in vision clear beheld
The sudden dark of tropic night shut down
O'er the huge whisper of great watery wastes,
The while a pair of herons trailingly
Flapped inland, where some league-wide river hurled
The yellow spoil of unconjectured realms
Far through a gulf's green silence, never scarred
By any but the North-wind's hurrying keels.
And not the pines alone; all sights and sounds
To my world-seeking heart paid fealty,
And catered for it as the Cretan bees
Brought honey to the baby Jupiter,
Who in his soft hand crushed a violet,
Godlike foremusing the rough thunder's gripe;
Then did I entertain the poet's song,
My great Idea's guest, and, passing o'er
That iron bridge the Tuscan built to hell,
I heard Ulysses tell of mountain-chains
Whose adamantine links, his manacles,
The western main shook growling, and still gnawed.

I brooded on the wise Athenian's tale
Of happy Atlantis, and heard Björne's keel
Crunch the gray pebbles of the Vinland shore :
I listened, musing, to the prophecy
Of Nero's tutor-victim ; lo, the birds
Sing darkling, conscious of the climbing dawn.
And I believed the poets ; it is they
Who utter wisdom from the central deep,
And, listening to the inner flow of things,
Speak to the age out of eternity.

Ah me ! old hermits sought for solitude
In caves and desert places of the earth,
Where their own heart-beat was the only stir
Of living thing that comforted the year ;
But the bald pillar-top of Simeon,
In midnight's blankest waste, were populous,
Matched with the isolation drear and deep
Of him who pines among the swarm of men,
At once a new thought's king and prisoner,
Feeling the truer life within his life,
The fountain of his spirit's prophecy,
Sinking away and wasting, drop by drop,
In the ungrateful sands of sceptic ears.
He in the palace-aisles of untrod woods
Doth walk a king ; for him the pent-up cell
Widens beyond the circles of the stars,
And all the sceptred spirits of the past
Come thronging in to greet him as their peer ;
But in the market-place's glare and throng
He sits apart, an exile, and his brow
Aches with the mocking memory of its crown.

I

Yet to the spirit select there is no choice;
He cannot say, This will I do, or that,
For the cheap means putting Heaven's ends in pawn,
And bartering his bleak rocks, the freehold stern
Of destiny's first-born, for smoother fields
That yield no crop of self-denying will;
A hand is stretched to him from out the dark,
Which grasping without question, he is led
Where there is work that he must do for God.
The trial still is the strength's complement,
And the uncertain, dizzy path that scales
The sheer heights of supremest purposes
Is steeper to the angel than the child.
Chances have laws as fixed as planets have,
And disappointment's dry and bitter root,
Envy's harsh berries, and the choking pool
Of the world's scorn, are the right mother-milk
To the tough hearts that pioneer their kind,
And break a pathway to those unknown realms
That in the earth's broad shadow lie enthralled;
Endurance is the crowning quality,
And patience all the passion of great hearts;
These are their stay, and when the leaden world
Sets its hard face against their fateful thought,
And brute strength, like the Gaulish conqueror,
Clangs his huge glaive down in the other scale,
The inspired soul but flings his patience in,
And slowly that outweighs the ponderous globe, —
One faith against a whole earth's unbelief,
One soul against the flesh of all mankind.

Thus ever seems it when my soul can hear

The voice that errs not; then my triumph gleams,
O'er the blank ocean beckoning, and all night
My heart flies on before me as I sail;
Far on I see my lifelong enterprise,
That rose like Ganges mid the freezing snows
Of a world's solitude, sweep broadening down,
And, gathering to itself a thousand streams,
Grow sacred ere it mingle with the sea;
I see the ungated wall of chaos old,
With blocks Cyclopean hewn of solid night,
Fade like a wreath of unreturning mist
Before the irreversible feet of light; —
And lo, with what clear omen in the east
On day's gray threshold stands the eager dawn,
Like young Leander rosy from the sea
Glowing at Hero's lattice!
                                    One day more
These muttering Shoalbrains leave the helm to me:
God, let me not in their dull ooze be stranded;
Let not this one frail bark, to hollow which
I have dug out the pith and sinewy heart
Of my aspiring life's fair trunk, be so
Cast up to warp and blacken in the sun,
Just as the opposing wind 'gins whistle off
His cheek-swollen pack, and from the leaning mast
Fortune's full sail strains forward!

                                    One poor day! —
Remember whose and not how short it is!
It is God's day, it is Columbus's.
A lavish day! One day, with life and heart,
Is more than time enough to find a world.

AN INCIDENT OF THE FIRE AT HAMBURG

THE tower of old Saint Nicholas soared upward to
    the skies,
Like some huge piece of Nature's make, the growth
    of centuries;
You could not deem its crowding spires a work of
    human art,
They seemed to struggle lightward from a sturdy
    living heart.

Not Nature's self more freely speaks in crystal or in
    oak,
Than, through the pious builder's hand, in that gray
    pile she spoke;
And as from acorn springs the oak, so, freely and
    alone,
Sprang from his heart this hymn to God, sung in
    obedient stone.

It seemed a wondrous freak of chance, so perfect,
    yet so rough,
A whim of Nature crystallized slowly in granite
    tough;
The thick spires yearned towards the sky in quaint
    harmonious lines,
And in broad sunlight basked and slept, like a grove
    of blasted pines.

Never did rock or stream or tree lay claim with
    better right
To all the adorning sympathies of shadow and of
    light;
And, in that forest petrified, as forester there dwells
Stout Herman, the old sacristan, sole lord of all its bells.

Surge leaping after surge, the fire roared onward red
    as blood,
Till half of Hamburg lay engulfed beneath the eddy-
    ing flood;
For miles away the fiery spray poured down its
    deadly rain,
And back and forth the billows sucked, and paused,
    and burst again.

From square to square with tiger leaps panted the lust-
    ful fire,
The air to leeward shuddered with the gasps of its
    desire;
And church and palace, which even now stood
    whelmed but to the knee,
Lift their black roofs like breakers lone amid the
    whirling sea.

Up in his tower old Herman sat and watched with
    quiet look;
His soul had trusted God too long to be at last forsook;
He could not fear, for surely God a pathway would
    unfold
Through this red sea for faithful hearts, as once He
    did of old.

But scarcely can he cross himself, or on his good
  saint call,
Before the sacrilegious flood o'erleaped the churchyard wall;
And, ere a *pater* half was said, mid smoke and
  crackling glare,
His island tower scarce juts its head above the wide
  despair.

Upon the peril's desperate peak his heart stood up
  sublime;
His first thought was for God above, his next was
  for his chime;
" Sing now and make your voices heard in hymns
  of praise," cried he,
" As did the Israelites of old, safe walking through
  the sea !

" Through this red sea our God hath made the pathway safe to shore;
Our promised land stands full in sight; shout now
  as ne'er before! "
And as the tower came crashing down, the bells,
  in clear accord,
Pealed forth the grand old German hymn, — " All
  good souls, praise the Lord ! "

THE SOWER

I saw a Sower walking slow
Across the earth, from east to west;
His hair was white as mountain snow,
His head drooped forward on his breast.

With shrivelled hands he flung his seed,
Nor ever turned to look behind;
Of sight or sound he took no heed;
It seemed he was both deaf and blind.

His dim face showed no soul beneath,
Yet in my heart I felt a stir,
As if I looked upon the sheath,
That once had held Excalibur.

I heard, as still the seed he cast,
How, crooning to himself, he sung,
"I sow again the holy Past,
The happy days when I was young.

"Then all was wheat without a tare,
Then all was righteous, fair, and true;
And I am he whose thoughtful care
Shall plant the Old World in the New.

" The fruitful germs I scatter free,
With busy hand, while all men sleep;
In Europe now, from sea to sea,
The nations bless me as they reap."

Then I looked back along his path,
And heard the clash of steel on steel,
Where man faced man, in deadly wrath,
While clanged the tocsin's hurrying peal.

The sky with burning towns flared red,
Nearer the noise of fighting rolled,
And brothers' blood, by brothers shed,
Crept curdling over pavements cold.

Then marked I how each germ of truth
Which through the dotard's fingers ran
Was mated with a dragon's tooth
Whence there sprang up an armëd man.

I shouted, but he could not hear;
Made signs, but these he could not see;
And still, without a doubt or fear,
Broadcast he scattered anarchy.

Long to my straining ears the blast
Brought faintly back the words he sung:
" I sow again the holy Past,
The happy days when I was young."

HUNGER AND COLD

SISTERS two, all praise to you,
With your faces pinched and blue;
To the poor man you 've been true
        From of old :
You can speak the keenest word,
You are sure of being heard,
From the point you 're never stirred,
        Hunger and Cold !

Let sleek statesmen temporize ;
Palsied are their shifts and lies
When they meet your bloodshot eyes,
        Grim and bold ;
Policy you set at naught,
In their traps you 'll not be caught,
You 're too honest to be bought,
        Hunger and Cold !

Bolt and bar the palace door ;
While the mass of men are poor,
Naked truth grows more and more
        Uncontrolled ;
You had never yet, I guess,
Any praise for bashfulness,
You can visit sans court-dress,
        Hunger and Cold !

While the music fell and rose,
And the dance reeled to its close,
Where her round of costly woes
    Fashion strolled,
I beheld with shuddering fear
Wolves' eyes through the windows peer;
Little dream they you are near,
    Hunger and Cold!

When the toiler's heart you clutch,
Conscience is not valued much,
He recks not a bloody smutch
    On his gold:
Everything to you defers,
You are potent reasoners,
At your whisper Treason stirs,
    Hunger and Cold!

Rude comparisons you draw,
Words refuse to sate your maw,
Your gaunt limbs the cobweb law
    Cannot hold:
You're not clogged with foolish pride,
But can seize a right denied:
Somehow God is on your side,
    Hunger and Cold!

You respect no hoary wrong
More for having triumphed long;
Its past victims, haggard throng,
    From the mould

You unbury : swords and spears
Weaker are than poor men's tears,
Weaker than your silent years,
    Hunger and Cold !

Let them guard both hall and bower;
Through the window you will glower,
Patient till your reckoning hour
    Shall be tolled ;
Cheeks are pale, but hands are red,
Guiltless blood may chance be shed,
But ye must and will be fed,
    Hunger and Cold !

God has plans man must not spoil,
Some were made to starve and toil,
Some to share the wine and oil,
    We are told :
Devil's theories are these,
Stifling hope and love and peace,
Framed your hideous lusts to please,
    Hunger and Cold !

Scatter ashes on thy head,
Tears of burning sorrow shed,
Earth ! and be by Pity led
    To Love's fold ;
Ere they block the very door
With lean corpses of the poor,
And will hush for naught but gore,
    Hunger and Cold !

THE LANDLORD

WHAT boot your houses and your lands ?
   In spite of close-drawn deed and fence,
Like water, 'twixt your cheated hands,
They slip into the graveyard's sands,
   And mock your ownership's pretence.

How shall you speak to urge your right,
   Choked with that soil for which you lust ?
The bit of clay, for whose delight
You grasp, is mortgaged, too ; Death might
   Foreclose this very day in dust.

Fence as you please, this plain poor man,
   Whose only fields are in his wit,
Who shapes the world, as best he can,
According to God's higher plan,
   Owns you, and fences as is fit.

Though yours the rents, his incomes wax
   By right of eminent domain ;
From factory tall to woodman's axe,
All things on earth must pay their tax,
   To feed his hungry heart and brain.

He takes you from your easy-chair,
   And what he plans that you must do ;
You sleep in down, eat dainty fare, —
He mounts his crazy garret-stair
   And starves, the landlord over you.

Feeding the clods your idlesse drains,
    You make more green six feet of soil;
His fruitful word, like suns and rains,
Partakes the seasons' bounteous pains,
    And toils to lighten human toil.

Your lands, with force or cunning got,
    Shrink to the measure of the grave;
But Death himself abridges not
The tenures of almighty thought,
    The titles of the wise and brave.

TO A PINE-TREE

FAR up on Katahdin thou towerest,
    Purple-blue with the distance and vast;
Like a cloud o'er the lowlands thou lowerest,
    That hangs poised on a lull in the blast,
        To its fall leaning awful.

In the storm, like a prophet o'ermaddened,
    Thou singest and tossest thy branches;
Thy heart with the terror is gladdened,
    Thou forebodest the dread avalanches,
        When whole mountains swoop valeward.

In the calm thou o'erstretchest the valleys
    With thine arms, as if blessings imploring,
Like an old king led forth from his palace,
    When his people to battle are pouring
        From the city beneath him.

To the lumberer asleep 'neath thy glooming
  Thou dost sing of wild billows in motion,
Till he longs to be swung mid their booming
  In the tents of the Arabs of ocean,
    Whose finned isles are their cattle.

For the gale snatches thee for his lyre,
  With mad hand crashing melody frantic,
While he pours forth his mighty desire
  To leap down on the eager Atlantic,
    Whose arms stretch to his playmate.

The wild storm makes his lair in thy branches,
  Swooping thence on the continent under;
Like a lion, crouched close on his haunches,
  There awaiteth his leap the fierce thunder,
    Growling low with impatience.

Spite of winter, thou keep'st thy green glory,
  Lusty father of Titans past number!
The snowflakes alone make thee hoary,
  Nestling close to thy branches in slumber,
    And thee mantling with silence.

Thou alone know'st the splendor of winter,
  Mid thy snow-silvered, hushed precipices,
Hearing crags of green ice groan and splinter,
  And then plunge down the muffled abysses
    In the quiet of midnight.

Thou alone know'st the glory of summer,
   Gazing down on thy broad seas of forest,
On thy subjects that send a proud murmur
   Up to thee, to their sachem, who towerest
     From thy bleak throne to heaven.

SI DESCENDERO IN INFERNUM, ADES

O, WANDERING dim on the extremest edge
   Of God's bright providence, whose spirits sigh
Drearily in you, like the winter sedge
   That shivers o'er the dead pool stiff and dry,
   A thin, sad voice, when the bold wind roars by
     From the clear North of Duty, —
Still by cracked arch and broken shaft I trace
That here was once a shrine and holy place
     Of the supernal Beauty,
   A child's play-altar reared of stones and moss,
   With wilted flowers for offering laid across,
Mute recognition of the all-ruling Grace.

How far are ye from the innocent, from those
   Whose hearts are as a little lane serene,
Smooth-heaped from wall to wall with unbroke snows,
   Or in the summer blithe with lamb-cropped green,
   Save the one track, where naught more rude is
     seen
     Than the plump wain at even
Bringing home four months' sunshine bound in
     sheaves !

How far are ye from those ! yet who believes
    That ye can shut out heaven ?
  Your souls partake its influence, not in vain
  Nor all unconscious, as that silent lane
Its drift of noiseless apple-blooms receives.

Looking within myself, I note how thin
  A plank of station, chance, or prosperous fate,
Doth fence me from the clutching waves of sin ;
  In my own heart I find the worst man's mate,
  And see not dimly the smooth-hingëd gate
    That opes to those abysses
Where ye grope darkly, — ye who never knew
On your young hearts love's consecrating dew,
    Or felt a mother's kisses,
  Or home's restraining tendrils round you curled ;
  Ah, side by side with heart's-ease in this world
The fatal nightshade grows and bitter rue !

One band ye cannot break, — the force that clips
  And grasps your circles to the central light ;
Yours is the prodigal comet's long ellipse,
  Self-exiled to the farthest verge of night ;
    Yet strives with you no less that inward might
    No sin hath e'er imbruted ;
The god in you the creed-dimmed eye eludes ;
The Law brooks not to have its solitudes
    By bigot feet polluted ;
    Yet they who watch your God-compelled return
    May see your happy perihelion burn
Where the calm sun his unfledged planets broods.

TO THE PAST

WONDROUS and awful are thy silent halls,
    O kingdom of the past!
There lie the bygone ages in their palls,
    Guarded by shadows vast;
  There all is hushed and breathless,
Save when some image of old error falls
  Earth worshipped once as deathless.

There sits drear Egypt, mid beleaguering sands,
    Half woman and half beast,
The burnt-out torch within her mouldering hands
    That once lit all the East;
  A dotard bleared and hoary,
There Asser crouches o'er the blackened brands
  Of Asia's long-quenched glory.

Still as a city buried 'neath the sea
    Thy courts and temples stand;
Idle as forms on wind-waved tapestry
    Of saints and heroes grand,
  Thy phantasms grope and shiver,
Or watch the loose shores crumbling silently
  Into Time's gnawing river.

Titanic shapes with faces blank and dun,
    Of their old godhead lorn,
Gaze on the embers of the sunken sun,
    Which they misdeem for morn;

I

And yet the eternal sorrow
In their unmonarched eyes says day is done
　Without the hope of morrow.

O realm of silence and of swart eclipse,
　　The shapes that haunt thy gloom
Make signs to us and move their withered lips
　　Across the gulf of doom ;
　　Yet all their sound and motion
Bring no more freight to us than wraiths of ships
　On the mirage's ocean.

And if sometimes a moaning wandereth
　　From out thy desolate halls,
If some grim shadow of thy living death
　　Across our sunshine falls
　　And scares the world to error,
The eternal life sends forth melodious breath
　To chase the misty terror.

Thy mighty clamors, wars, and world-noised deeds
　　Are silent now in dust,
Gone like a tremble of the huddling reeds
　　Beneath some sudden gust ;
　　Thy forms and creeds have vanished,
Tossed out to wither like unsightly weeds
　From the world's garden banished.

Whatever of true life there was in thee
　　Leaps in our age's veins ;
Wield still thy bent and wrinkled empery,
　　And shake thine idle chains ; —

To thee thy dross is clinging,
For us thy martyrs die, thy prophets see,
Thy poets still are singing.

Here, mid the bleak waves of our strife and care,
Float the green Fortunate Isles
Where all thy hero-spirits dwell, and share
Our martyrdoms and toils;
The present moves attended
With all of brave and excellent and fair
That made the old time splendid.

TO THE FUTURE

O LAND of Promise! from what Pisgah's height
Can I behold thy stretch of peaceful bowers,
Thy golden harvests flowing out of sight,
Thy nestled homes and sun-illumined towers?
Gazing upon the sunset's high-heaped gold,
Its crags of opal and of chrysolite,
Its deeps on deeps of glory, that unfold
Still brightening abysses,
And blazing precipices,
Whence but a scanty leap it seems to heaven,
Sometimes a glimpse is given
Of thy more gorgeous realm, thy more unstinted
blisses.

O Land of Quiet! to thy shore the surf
Of the perturbëd Present rolls and sleeps;

Our storms breathe soft as June upon thy turf
  And lure out blossoms; to thy bosom leaps,
As to a mother's, the o'erwearied heart,
Hearing far off and dim the toiling mart,
    The hurrying feet, the curses without number,
      And, circled with the glow Elysian
      Of thine exulting vision,
Out of its very cares wooes charms for peace and
      slumber.

To thee the earth lifts up her fettered hands
  And cries for vengeance; with a pitying smile
Thou blessest her, and she forgets her bands,
  And her old woe-worn face a little while
Grows young and noble; unto thee the Oppressor
      Looks, and is dumb with awe;
      The eternal law,
Which makes the crime its own blindfold redresser,
Shadows his heart with perilous foreboding,
      And he can see the grim-eyed Doom
      From out the trembling gloom
Its silent-footed steeds towards his palace goading.

What promises hast thou for Poets' eyes,
  Aweary of the turmoil and the wrong!
To all their hopes what overjoyed replies!
  What undreamed ecstasies for blissful song!
Thy happy plains no war-trump's brawling clangor
  Disturbs, and fools the poor to hate the poor;
The humble glares not on the high with anger;
    Love leaves no grudge at less, no greed for
      more;

In vain strives Self the godlike sense to smother;
    From the soul's deeps
    It throbs and leaps;
The noble 'neath foul rags beholds his long-lost
    brother.

To thee the Martyr looketh, and his fires
    Unlock their fangs and leave his spirit free;
To thee the Poet mid his toil aspires,
    And grief and hunger climb about his knee,
Welcome as children; thou upholdest
    The lone Inventor by his demon haunted;
The Prophet cries to thee when hearts are coldest,
    And gazing o'er the midnight's bleak abyss,
    Sees the drowsed soul awaken at thy kiss,
And stretch its happy arms and leap up disenchanted.

Thou bringest vengeance, but so loving-kindly
    The guilty thinks it pity; taught by thee,
Fierce tyrants drop the scourges wherewith blindly
    Their own souls they were scarring; conquerors see
With horror in their hands the accursed spear
    That tore the meek One's side on Calvary,
And from their trophies shrink with ghastly fear;
    Thou, too, art the Forgiver,
    The beauty of man's soul to man revealing;
    The arrows from thy quiver
Pierce Error's guilty heart, but only pierce for healing.

Oh, whither, whither, glory-wingēd dreams,
    From out Life's sweat and turmoil would ye bear me?
Shut, gates of Fancy, on your golden gleams, —
    This agony of hopeless contrast spare me!

Fade, cheating glow, and leave me to my night!
  He is a coward, who would borrow
  A charm against the present sorrow
From the vague Future's promise of delight:
  As life's alarums nearer roll,
    The ancestral buckler calls,
    Self-clanging from the walls
  In the high temple of the soul;
Where are most sorrows, there the poet's sphere is,
    To feed the soul with patience,
    To heal its desolations
With words of unshorn truth, with love that never
    wearies.

HEBE

  I saw the twinkle of white feet,
I saw the flash of robes descending;
  Before her ran an influence fleet,
That bowed my heart like barley bending.

  As, in bare fields, the searching bees
Pilot to blooms beyond our finding,
  It led me on, by sweet degrees
Joy's simple honey-cells unbinding.

  Those Graces were that seemed grim Fates;
With nearer love the sky leaned o'er me;
  The long-sought Secret's golden gates
On musical hinges swung before me.

I saw the brimmed bowl in her grasp
Thrilling with godhood; like a lover
  I sprang the proffered life to clasp;—
The beaker fell; the luck was over.

  The Earth has drunk the vintage up;
What boots it patch the goblet's splinters?
  Can Summer fill the icy cup,
Whose treacherous crystal is but Winter's?

  O spendthrift haste! await the Gods;
Their nectar crowns the lips of Patience;
  Haste scatters on unthankful sods
The immortal gift in vain libations.

  Coy Hebe flies from those that woo,
And shuns the hands would seize upon her;
  Follow thy life, and she will sue
To pour for thee the cup of honor.

THE SEARCH

  I WENT to seek for Christ,
  And Nature seemed so fair
That first the woods and fields my youth enticed,
  And I was sure to find him there:
    The temple I forsook,
    And to the solitude
Allegiance paid; but Winter came and shook
  The crown and purple from my wood;

His snows, like desert sands, with scornful drift,
  Besieged the columned aisle and palace-gate;
My Thebes, cut deep with many a solemn rift,
  But epitaphed her own sepulchred state:
Then I remembered whom I went to seek,
And blessed blunt Winter for his counsel bleak.

  Back to the world I turned,
    For Christ, I said, is King;
So the cramped alley and the hut I spurned,
    As far beneath his sojourning:
      Mid power and wealth I sought,
      But found no trace of him,
And all the costly offerings I had brought
    With sudden rust and mould grew dim:
I found his tomb, indeed, where, by their laws,
  All must on stated days themselves imprison,
Mocking with bread a dead creed's grinning jaws,
  Witless how long the life had thence arisen;
Due sacrifice to this they set apart,
Prizing it more than Christ's own living heart.

    So from my feet the dust
    Of the proud World I shook;
Then came dear Love and shared with me his crust,
    And half my sorrow's burden took.
      After the World's soft bed,
      Its rich and dainty fare,
Like down seemed Love's coarse pillow to my head,
      His cheap food seemed as manna rare;
Fresh-trodden prints of bare and bleeding feet,
  Turned to the heedless city whence I came,

Hard by I saw, and springs of worship sweet
  Gushed from my cleft heart smitten by the same;
Love looked me in the face and spake no words,
But straight I knew those footprints were the Lord's.

     I followed where they led,
     And in a hovel rude,
With naught to fence the weather from his head,
    The King I sought for meekly stood;
     A naked, hungry child
     Clung round his gracious knee,
And a poor hunted slave looked up and smiled
    To bless the smile that set him free;
New miracles I saw his presence do, —
   No more I knew the hovel bare and poor,
The gathered chips into a woodpile grew,
   The broken morsel swelled to goodly store;
I knelt and wept: my Christ no more I seek,
His throne is with the outcast and the weak.

THE PRESENT CRISIS

WHEN a deed is done for Freedom, through the broad
     earth's aching breast
Runs a thrill of joy prophetic, trembling on from east
     to west,
And the slave, where'er he cowers, feels the soul
     within him climb
To the awful verge of manhood, as the energy sublime
Of a century bursts full-blossomed on the thorny stem
     of Time.

Through the walls of hut and palace shoots the instantaneous throe,
When the travail of the Ages wrings earth's systems to and fro;
At the birth of each new Era, with a recognizing start,
Nation wildly looks at nation, standing with mute lips apart,
And glad Truth's yet mightier man-child leaps beneath the Future's heart.

So the Evil's triumph sendeth, with a terror and a chill,
Under continent to continent, the sense of coming ill,
And the slave, where'er he cowers, feels his sympathies with God
In hot tear-drops ebbing earthward, to be drunk up by the sod,
Till a corpse crawls round unburied, delving in the nobler clod.

For mankind are one in spirit, and an instinct bears along,
Round the earth's electric circle, the swift flash of right or wrong;
Whether conscious or unconscious, yet Humanity's vast frame
Through its ocean-sundered fibres feels the gush of joy or shame; —
In the gain or loss of one race all the rest have equal claim.

Once to every man and nation comes the moment to
    decide,
In the strife of Truth with Falsehood, for the good or
    evil side;
Some great cause, God's new Messiah, offering each
    the bloom or blight,
Parts the goats upon the left hand, and the sheep upon
    the right,
And the choice goes by forever 'twixt that darkness
    and that light.

Hast thou chosen, O my people, on whose party thou
    shalt stand,
Ere the Doom from its worn sandals shakes the dust
    against our land?
Though the cause of Evil prosper, yet 't is Truth
    alone is strong,
And, albeit she wander outcast now, I see around her
    throng
Troops of beautiful, tall angels, to enshield her from
    all wrong.

Backward look across the ages and the beacon-mo-
    ments see,
That, like peaks of some sunk continent, jut through
    Oblivion's sea;
Not an ear in court or market for the low foreboding
    cry
Of those Crises, God's stern winnowers, from whose
    feet earth's chaff must fly;
Never shows the choice momentous till the judgment
    hath passed by.

Careless seems the great Avenger; history's pages but
    record
One death-grapple in the darkness 'twixt old systems
    and the Word;
Truth forever on the scaffold, Wrong forever on the
    throne, —
Yet that scaffold sways the future, and, behind the
    dim unknown,
Standeth God within the shadow, keeping watch above
    his own.

We see dimly in the Present what is small and what
    is great,
Slow of faith how weak an arm may turn the iron
    helm of fate,
But the soul is still oracular; amid the market's
    din,
List the ominous stern whisper from the Delphic cave
    within, —
" They enslave their children's children who make
    compromise with sin."

Slavery, the earth-born Cyclops, fellest of the giant
    brood,
Sons of brutish Force and Darkness, who have
    drenched the earth with blood,
Famished in his self-made desert, blinded by our purer
    day,
Gropes in yet unblasted regions for his miserable
    prey; —
Shall we guide his gory fingers where our helpless chil-
    dren play?

Then to side with Truth is noble when we share her
      wretched crust,
Ere her cause bring fame and profit, and 't is prosper-
      ous to be just;
Then it is the brave man chooses, while the coward
      stands aside,
Doubting in his abject spirit, till his Lord is cruci-
      fied,
And the multitude make virtue of the faith they had
      denied.

Count me o 'er earth's chosen heroes, — they were
      souls that stood alone,
While the men they agonized for hurled the contu-
      melious stone,
Stood serene, and down the future saw the golden
      beam incline
To the side of perfect justice, mastered by their faith
      divine,
By one man's plain truth to manhood and to God's
      supreme design.

By the light of burning heretics Christ's bleeding feet
      I track,
Toiling up new Calvaries ever with the cross that
      turns not back,
And these mounts of anguish number how each gen-
      eration learned
One new word of that grand *Credo* which in prophct-
      hearts hath burned
Since the first man stood God-conquered with his
      face to heaven upturned.

For Humanity sweeps onward : where to-day the
    martyr stands,
On the morrow crouches Judas with the silver in his
    hands ;
Far in front the cross stands ready and the crackling
    fagots burn,
While the hooting mob of yesterday in silent awe
    return
To glean up the scattered ashes into History's golden
    urn.

'Tis as easy to be heroes as to sit the idle slaves
Of a legendary virtue carved upon our fathers'
    graves,
Worshippers of light ancestral make the present light
    a crime ; —
Was the Mayflower launched by cowards, steered by
    men behind their time ?
Turn those tracks toward Past or Future, that make
    Plymouth Rock sublime ?

They were men of present valor, stalwart old icon-
    oclasts,
Unconvinced by axe or gibbet that all virtue was the
    Past's ;
But we make their truth our falsehood, thinking that
    hath made us free,
Hoarding it in mouldy parchments, while our tender
    spirits flee
The rude grasp of that great Impulse which drove
    them across the sea.

They have rights who dare maintain them ; we are
    traitors to our sires,
Smothering in their holy ashes Freedom's new-lit
    altar-fires ;
Shall we make their creed our jailer ? Shall we, in our
    haste to slay,
From the tombs of the old prophets steal the funeral
    lamps away
To light up the martyr-fagots round the prophets of
    to-day ?

New occasions teach new duties ; Time makes an-
    cient good uncouth ;
They must upward still, and onward, who would keep
    abreast of Truth ;
Lo, before us gleam her camp-fires ! we ourselves
    must Pilgrims be,
Launch our Mayflower, and steer boldly through the
    desperate winter sea,
Nor attempt the Future's portal with the Past's blood-
    rusted key.

December, 1844.

AN INDIAN–SUMMER REVERIE

WHAT visionary tints the year puts on,
When falling leaves falter through motionless air,
    Or numbly cling and shiver to be gone !
How shimmer the low flats and pastures bare,

As with her nectar Hebe Autumn fills
The bowl between me and those distant hills,
And smiles and shakes abroad her misty, tremulous
        hair !

No more the landscape holds its wealth apart,
    Making me poorer in my poverty,
        But mingles with my senses and my heart;
    My own projected spirit seems to me
        In her own reverie the world to steep;
        'T is she that waves to sympathetic sleep,
Moving, as she is moved, each field and hill and tree.

How fuse and mix, with what unfelt degrees,
    Clasped by the faint horizon's languid arms,
        Each into each, the hazy distances !
    The softened season all the landscape charms;
        Those hills, my native village that embay,
        In waves of dreamier purple roll away,
And floating in mirage seem all the glimmering farms.

Far distant sounds the hidden chickadee
    Close at my side ; far distant sound the leaves ;
        The fields seem fields of dream, where Memory
Wanders like gleaning Ruth ; and as the sheaves
        Of wheat and barley wavered in the eye
        Of Boaz as the maiden's glow went by,
So tremble and seem remote all things the sense re-
        ceives.

The cock's shrill trump that tells of scattered
        corn,
Passed breezily on by all his flapping mates,

Faint and more faint, from barn to barn is borne,
Southward, perhaps to far Magellan's Straits;
  Dimly I catch the throb of distant flails;
  Silently overhead the hen-hawk sails,
With watchful, measuring eye, and for his quarry
      waits.

  The sobered robin, hunger-silent now,
Seeks cedar-berries blue, his autumn cheer;
  The chipmunk, on the shingly shagbark's bough,
Now saws, now lists with downward eye and ear,
  Then drops his nut, and, cheeping, with a bound
  Whisks to his winding fastness underground;
The clouds like swans drift down the streaming at-
      mosphere.

  O'er yon bare knoll the pointed cedar shadows
Drowse on the crisp, gray moss; the ploughman's
      call
  Creeps faint as smoke from black, fresh-furrowed
      meadows;
  The single crow a single caw lets fall;
  And all around me every bush and tree
  Says Autumn's here, and Winter soon will be,
Who snows his soft, white sleep and silence over all.

  The birch, most shy and ladylike of trees,
Her poverty, as best she may, retrieves,
  And hints at her foregone gentilities
With some saved relics of her wealth of leaves;
  The swamp-oak, with his royal purple on,
  Glares red as blood across the sinking sun,
As one who proudlier to a falling fortune cleaves.

I

He looks a sachem, in red blanket wrapt,
Who, mid some council of the sad-garbed whites,
Erect and stern, in his own memories lapt,
With distant eye broods over other sights,
Sees the hushed wood the city's flare replace,
The wounded turf heal o'er the railway's trace,
And roams the savage Past of his undwindled rights.

The red-oak, softer-grained, yields all for lost,
And, with his crumpled foliage stiff and dry,
After the first betrayal of the frost,
Rebuffs the kiss of the relenting sky;
The chestnuts, lavish of their long-hid gold,
To the faint Summer, beggared now and old,
Pour back the sunshine hoarded 'neath her favoring
eye.

The ash her purple drops forgivingly
And sadly, breaking not the general hush;
The maple-swamps glow like a sunset sea,
Each leaf a ripple with its separate flush;
All round the wood's edge creeps the skirting
blaze
Of bushes low, as when, on cloudy days,
Ere the rain fall, the cautious farmer burns his brush.

O'er yon low wall, which guards one unkempt
zone,
Where vines and weeds and scrub-oaks intertwine
Safe from the plough, whose rough, discordant
stone
Is massed to one soft gray by lichens fine,

The tangled blackberry, crossed and recrossed,
    weaves
  A prickly network of ensanguined leaves;
Hard by, with coral beads, the prim black-alders shine.

  Pillaring with flame this crumbling boundary,
  Whose loose blocks topple 'neath the plough-boy's
    foot,
   Who, with each sense shut fast except the eye,
  Creeps close and scares the jay he hoped to shoot,
    The woodbine up the elm's straight stem as-
      spires,
    Coiling it, harmless, with autumnal fires;
In the ivy's paler blaze the martyr oak stands mute.

  Below, the Charles, a stripe of nether sky,
  Now hid by rounded apple-trees between,
    Whose gaps the misplaced sail sweeps bellying by,
  Now flickering golden through a woodland screen,
    Then spreading out, at his next turn beyond,
    A silver circle like an inland pond —
Slips seaward silently through marshes purple and
    green.

  Dear marshes! vain to him the gift of sight
  Who cannot in their various incomes share,
    From every season drawn, of shade and light,
  Who sees in them but levels brown and bare;
    Each change of storm or sunshine scatters free
    On them its largess of variety,
For Nature with cheap means still works her wonders
    rare.

In Spring they lie one broad expanse of green,
O'er which the light winds run with glimmering
feet :
Here, yellower stripes track out the creek un-
seen,
There, darker growths o'er hidden ditches meet ;
And purpler stains show where the blossoms
crowd,
As if the silent shadow of a cloud
Hung there becalmed, with the next breath to fleet.

All round, upon the river's slippery edge,
Witching to deeper calm the drowsy tide,
Whispers and leans the breeze-entangling sedge ;
Through emerald glooms the lingering waters slide,
Or, sometimes wavering, throw back the sun,
And the stiff banks in eddies melt and run
Of dimpling light, and with the current seem to glide.

In Summer 't is a blithesome sight to see,
As, step by step, with measured swing, they pass,
The wide-ranked mowers wading to the knee,
Their sharp scythes panting through the wiry grass ;
Then, stretched beneath a rick's shade in a ring,
Their nooning take, while one begins to sing
A stave that droops and dies 'neath the close sky of
brass.

Meanwhile that devil-may-care, the bobolink,
Remembering duty, in mid-quaver stops
Just ere he sweeps o'er rapture's tremulous brink,
And 'twixt the winrows most demurely drops,

The Charles near Longfellow's House

A decorous bird of business, who provides
  For his brown mate and fledglings six besides,
And looks from right to left, a farmer mid his crops.

   Another change subdues them in the Fall,
  But saddens not ; they still show merrier tints,
   Though sober russet seems to cover all ;
  When the first sunshine through their dew-drops
    glints,
   Look how the yellow clearness, streamed across,
   Redeems with rarer hues the season's loss,
As Dawn's feet there had touched and left their rosy
   prints.

  Or come when sunset gives its freshened zest,
  Lean o'er the bridge and let the ruddy thrill,
   While the shorn sun swells down the hazy west,
  Glow opposite ; — the marshes drink their fill
   And swoon with purple veins, then slowly fade
   Through pink to brown, as eastward moves the
    shade,
Lengthening with stealthy creep, of Simond's darken-
   ing hill.

   Later, and yet ere Winter wholly shuts,
  Ere through the first dry snow the runner grates,
   And the loath cart-wheel screams in slippery ruts,
  While firmer ice the eager boy awaits,
   Trying each buckle and strap beside the fire,
   And until bedtime plays with his desire,
Twenty times putting on and off his new-bought
   skates ; —

Then, every morn, the river's banks shine bright
With smooth plate-armor, treacherous and frail,
    By the frost's clinking hammers forged at night,
'Gainst which the lances of the sun prevail,
    Giving a pretty emblem of the day
    When guiltier arms in light shall melt away,
And states shall move free-limbed, loosed from war's
        cramping mail.

    And now those waterfalls the ebbing river
  Twice every day creates on either side
      Tinkle, as through their fresh-sparred grots they
          shiver
  In grass-arched channels to the sun denied ;
      High flaps in sparkling blue the far-heard crow,
      The silvered flats gleam frostily below,
Suddenly drops the gull and breaks the glassy tide.

    But crowned in turn by vying seasons three,
  Their winter halo hath a fuller ring ;
      This glory seems to rest immovably, —
  The others were too fleet and vanishing ;
      When the hid tide is at its highest flow,
      O'er marsh and stream one breathless trance of
          snow
With brooding fulness awes and hushes everything.

    The sunshine seems blown off by the bleak wind,
  As pale as formal candles lit by day ;
      Gropes to the sea the river dumb and blind ;
  The brown ricks, snow-thatched by the storm in
      play,

Show pearly breakers combing o'er their lee,
White crests as of some just enchanted sea,
Checked in their maddest leap and hanging poised
  midway.

But when the eastern blow, with rain aslant,
From mid-sea's prairies green and rolling plains
  Drives in his wallowing herds of billows gaunt,
And the roused Charles remembers in his veins
  Old Ocean's blood and snaps his gyves of
    frost,
  That tyrannous silence on the shores is tost
In dreary wreck, and crumbling desolation reigns.

Edgewise or flat, in Druid-like device,
With leaden pools between or gullies bare,
  The blocks lie strewn, a bleak Stonehenge of
    ice;
No life, no sound, to break the grim despair,
  Save sullen plunge, as through the sedges stiff
  Down crackles riverward some thaw-sapped cliff,
Or when the close-wedged fields of ice crunch here
    and there.

But let me turn from fancy-pictured scenes
To that whose pastoral calm before me lies:
  Here nothing harsh or rugged intervenes;
The early evening with her misty dyes
  Smooths off the ravelled edges of the nigh,
  Relieves the distant with her cooler sky,
And tones the landscape down, and soothes the
    wearied eyes.

There gleams my native village, dear to me,
　Though higher change's waves each day are seen,
　　Whelming fields famed in boyhood's history,
　Sanding with houses the diminished green;
　　There, in red brick, which softening time defies,
　　Stand square and stiff the Muses' factories; —
How with my life knit up is every well-known scene!

Flow on, dear river! not alone you flow
　To outward sight, and through your marshes wind;
　　Fed from the mystic springs of long-ago,
　Your twin flows silent through my world of mind:
　　Grow dim, dear marshes, in the evening's gray!
　　Before my inner sight ye stretch away,
And will forever, though these fleshly eyes grow blind.

Beyond the hillock's house-bespotted swell,
　Where Gothic chapels house the horse and chaise,
　　Where quiet cits in Grecian temples dwell,
　Where Coptic tombs resound with prayer and praise,
　　Where dust and mud the equal year divide,
　　There gentle Allston lived, and wrought, and
　　　died,
Transfiguring street and shop with his illumined gaze.

Virgilium vidi tantum, — I have seen
　But as a boy, who looks alike on all,
　　That misty hair, that fine Undine-like mien,
　Tremulous as down to feeling's faintest call; —
　　Ah, dear old homestead! count it to thy fame
　　That thither many times the Painter came; —
One elm yet bears his name, a feathery tree and tall.

Swiftly the present fades in memory's glow, —
Our only sure possession is the past;
  The village blacksmith died a month ago,
And dim to me the forge's roaring blast;
  Soon fire-new mediævals we shall see
  Oust the black smithy from its chestnut-tree,
And that hewn down, perhaps, the bee-hive green and
    vast.

How many times, prouder than king on throne,
Loosed from the village school-dame's A's and B's,
  Panting have I the creaky bellows blown,
And watched the pent volcano's red increase,
  Then paused to see the ponderous sledge, brought
    down
  By that hard arm voluminous and brown,
From the white iron swarm its golden vanishing bees.

Dear native town! whose choking elms each year
With eddying dust before their time turn gray,
  Pining for rain, — to me thy dust is dear;
It glorifies the eve of summer day,
  And when the westering sun half sunken burns,
  The mote-thick air to deepest orange turns,
The westward horseman rides through clouds of gold
    away,

So palpable, I 've seen those unshorn few,
The six old willows at the causey's end
  (Such trees Paul Potter never dreamed nor drew),
Through this dry mist their checkering shadows
    send,

Striped, here and there, with many a long-drawn
    thread,
Where streamed through leafy chinks the trem-
    bling red,
Past which, in one bright trail, the hangbird's flashes
    blend.

Yes, dearer far thy dust than all that e'er,
Beneath the awarded crown of victory,
    Gilded the blown Olympic charioteer;
Though lightly prized the ribboned parchments
    three,
    Yet *collegisse juvat*, I am glad
    That here what colleging was mine I had, —
It linked another tie, dear native town, with thee!

Nearer art thou than simply native earth,
My dust with thine concedes a deeper tie;
    A closer claim thy soil may well put forth,
Something of kindred more than sympathy;
    For in thy bounds I reverently laid away
    That blinding anguish of forsaken clay,
That title I seemed to have in earth and sea and sky,

That portion of my life more choice to me
(Though brief, yet in itself so round and whole)
    Than all the imperfect residue can be;
The Artist saw his statue of the soul
    Was perfect; so, with one regretful stroke,
    The earthen model into fragments broke,
And without her the impoverished seasons roll.

THE GROWTH OF THE LEGEND

A FRAGMENT

A LEGEND that grew in the forest's hush
Slowly as tear-drops gather and gush,
When a word some poet chanced to say
Ages ago, in his careless way,
Brings our youth back to us out of its shroud
Clearly as under yon thunder-cloud
I see that white sea-gull. It grew and grew,
From the pine-trees gathering a sombre hue,
Till it seems a mere murmur out of the vast
Norwegian forests of the past;
And it grew itself like a true Northern pine,
First a little slender line,
Like a mermaid's green eyelash, and then anon
A stem that a tower might rest upon,
Standing spear-straight in the waist-deep moss,
Its bony roots clutching around and across,
As if they would tear up earth's heart in their grasp
Ere the storm should uproot them or make them
        unclasp;
Its cloudy boughs singing, as suiteth the pine,
To snow-bearded sea-kings old songs of the brine,
Till they straightened and let their staves fall to the
        floor,
Hearing waves moan again on the perilous shore
Of Vinland, perhaps, while their prow groped its way
'Twixt the frothed gnashing tusks of some ship-
        crunching bay.

So, pine-like, the legend grew, strong-limbed and tall,
As the Gypsy child grows that eats crusts in the hall;
It sucked the whole strength of the earth and the
      sky,
Spring, Summer, Fall, Winter, all brought it supply;
'T was a natural growth, and stood fearlessly there,
True part of the landscape as sea, land, and air;
For it grew in good times, ere the fashion it was
To force these wild births of the woods under glass,
And so, if 't is told as it should be told,
Though 't were sung under Venice's moonlight of
      gold,
You would hear the old voice of its mother, the pine,
Murmur sealike and northern through every line,
And the verses should grow, self-sustained and free,
Round the vibrating stem of the melody,
Like the lithe moonlit limbs of the parent tree.

Yes, the pine is the mother of legends; what food
For their grim roots is left when the thousand-yeared
      wood,
The dim-aisled cathedral, whose tall arches spring
Light, sinewy, graceful, firm-set as the wing
From Michael's white shoulder, is hewn and defaced
By iconoclast axes in desperate waste,
And its wrecks seek the ocean it prophesied long,
Cassandra-like, crooning its mystical song?
Then the legends go with them, — even yet on the
      sea
A wild virtue is left in the touch of the tree,
And the sailor's night-watches are thrilled to the core
With the lineal offspring of Odin and Thor.

Yes, wherever the pine-wood has never let in,
Since the day of creation, the light and the din
Of manifold life, but has safely conveyed
From the midnight primæval its armful of shade,
And has kept the weird Past with its child-faith
        alive
Mid the hum and the stir of To-day's busy hive,
There the legend takes root in the age-gathered gloom,
And its murmurous boughs for their sagas find room.

Where Aroostook, far-heard, seems to sob as he goes
Groping down to the sea 'neath his mountainous
        snows;
Where the lake's frore Sahara of never-tracked white,
When the crack shoots across it, complains to the
        night
With a long, lonely moan, that leagues northward is
        lost,
As the ice shrinks away from the tread of the frost;
Where the lumberers sit by the log-fires that throw
Their own threatening shadows far round o'er the
        snow,
When the wolf howls aloof, and the wavering glare
Flashes out from the blackness the eyes of the bear,
When the wood's huge recesses, half-lighted, supply
A canvas where Fancy her mad brush may try,
Blotting in giant Horrors that venture not down
Through the right-angled streets of the brisk, white-
        washed town,
But skulk in the depths of the measureless wood
Mid the Dark's creeping whispers that curdle the
        blood,

When the eye, glanced in dread o'er the shoulder, may
    dream,
Ere it shrinks to the camp-fire's companioning gleam,
That it saw the fierce ghost of the Red Man crouch
    back
To the shroud of the tree-trunk's invincible black;
There the old shapes crowd thick round the pine-
    shadowed camp,
Which shun the keen gleam of the scholarly lamp,
And the seed of the legend finds true Norland ground,
While the border-tale 's told and the canteen flits
    round.

A CONTRAST

THY love thou sentest oft to me,
    And still as oft I thrust it back ;
Thy messengers I could not see
    In those who everything did lack,
    The poor, the outcast, and the black.

Pride held his hand before mine eyes,
    The world with flattery stuffed mine ears ;
I looked to see a monarch's guise,
    Nor dreamed thy love would knock for years,
    Poor, naked, fettered, full of tears.

Yet, when I sent my love to thee,
    Thou with a smile didst take it in,

And entertain'dst it royally,
　　Though grimed with earth, with hunger thin,
　　And leprous with the taint of sin.

Now every day thy love I meet,
　　As o'er the earth it wanders wide,
With weary step and bleeding feet,
　　Still knocking at the heart of pride
　　And offering grace, though still denied.

EXTREME UNCTION

Go! leave me, Priest; my soul would be
　　Alone with the consoler, Death;
Far sadder eyes than thine will see
　　This crumbling clay yield up its breath;
These shrivelled hands have deeper stains
　　Than holy oil can cleanse away,
Hands that have plucked the world's coarse gains
　　As erst they plucked the flowers of May.

Call, if thou canst, to these gray eyes
　　Some faith from youth's traditions wrung;
This fruitless husk which dustward dries
　　Hath been a heart once, hath been young;
On this bowed head the awful Past
　　Once laid its consecrating hands;
The Future in its purpose vast
　　Paused, waiting my supreme commands.

But look! whose shadows block the door?
  Who are those two that stand aloof?
See! on my hands this freshening gore
  Writes o'er again its crimson proof!
My looked-for death-bed guests are met;
  There my dead Youth doth wring its hands,
And there, with eyes that goad me yet,
  The ghost of my Ideal stands!

God bends from out the deep and says,
  " I gave thee the great gift of life;
Wast thou not called in many ways?
  Are not my earth and heaven at strife?
I gave thee of my seed to sow,
  Bringest thou me my hundred-fold?"
Can I look up with face aglow,
  And answer, " Father, here is gold"?

I have been innocent; God knows
  When first this wasted life began,
Not grape with grape more kindly grows,
  Than I with every brother-man:
Now here I gasp; what lose my kind,
  When this fast ebbing breath shall part?
What bands of love and service bind
  This being to a brother heart?

Christ still was wandering o'er the earth
  Without a place to lay his head;
He found free welcome at my hearth,
  He shared my cup and broke my bread:

Now, when I hear those steps sublime,
    That bring the other world to this,
My snake-turned nature, sunk in slime,
    Starts sideway with defiant hiss.

Upon the hour when I was born,
    God said, " Another man shall be,"
And the great Maker did not scorn
    Out of himself to fashion me;
He sunned me with his ripening looks,
    And Heaven's rich instincts in me grew,
As effortless as woodland nooks
    Send violets up and paint them blue.

Yes, I who now, with angry tears,
    Am exiled back to brutish clod,
Have borne unquenched for fourscore years
    A spark of the eternal God ;
And to what end ? How yield I back
    The trust for such high uses given ?
Heaven's light hath but revealed a track
    Whereby to crawl away from heaven.

Men think it is an awful sight
    To see a soul just set adrift
On that drear voyage from whose night
    The ominous shadows never lift;
But 't is more awful to behold
    A helpless infant newly born,
Whose little hands unconscious hold
    The keys of darkness and of morn.

I

Mine held them once; I flung away
  Those keys that might have open set
The golden sluices of the day,
  But clutch the keys of darkness yet;
I hear the reapers singing go
  Into God's harvest; I, that might
With them have chosen, here below
  Grope shuddering at the gates of night.

O glorious Youth, that once wast mine!
  O high Ideal! all in vain
Ye enter at this ruined shrine
  Whence worship ne'er shall rise again;
The bat and owl inhabit here,
  The snake nests in the altar-stone,
The sacred vessels moulder near,
  The image of the God is gone.

THE OAK

WHAT gnarlëd stretch, what depth of shade, is
    his!
  There needs no crown to mark the forest's king;
How in his leaves outshines full summer's bliss!
  Sun, storm, rain, dew, to him their tribute bring,
Which he with such benignant royalty
  Accepts, as overpayeth what is lent;
All nature seems his vassal proud to be,
  And cunning only for his ornament.

How towers he, too, amid the billowed snows,
   An unquelled exile from the summer's throne,
Whose plain, uncinctured front more kingly shows,
   Now that the obscuring courtier leaves are flown.
His boughs make music of the winter air,
   Jewelled with sleet, like some cathedral front
Where clinging snow-flakes with quaint art repair
   The dints and furrows of time's envious brunt.

How doth his patient strength the rude March wind
   Persuade to seem glad breaths of summer breeze,
And win the soil that fain would be unkind,
   To swell his revenues with proud increase!
He is the gem; and all the landscape wide
   (So doth his grandeur isolate the sense)
Seems but the setting, worthless all beside,
   An empty socket, were he fallen thence.

So, from oft converse with life's wintry gales,
   Should man learn how to clasp with tougher roots
The inspiring earth; how otherwise avails
   The leaf-creating sap that sunward shoots?
So every year that falls with noiseless flake
   Should fill old scars up on the stormward side,
And make hoar age revered for age's sake,
   Not for traditions of youth's leafy pride.

So, from the pinched soil of a churlish fate,
   True hearts compel the sap of sturdier growth,
So between earth and heaven stand simply great,
   That these shall seem but their attendants both;

For Nature's forces with obedient zeal
    Wait on the rooted faith and oaken will;
As quickly the pretender's cheat they feel,
    And turn mad Pucks to flout and mock him still.

Lord! all thy works are lessons; each contains
    Some emblem of man's all-containing soul;
Shall he make fruitless all thy glorious pains,
    Delving within thy grace an eyeless mole?
Make me the least of thy Dodona-grove,
    Cause me some message of thy truth to bring,
Speak but a word through me, nor let thy love
    Among my boughs disdain to perch and sing.

AMBROSE

NEVER, surely, was holier man
Than Ambrose, since the world began;
With diet spare and raiment thin
He shielded himself from the father of sin;
With bed of iron and scourgings oft,
His heart to God's hand as wax made soft.

Through earnest prayer and watchings long
He sought to know 'tween right and wrong,
Much wrestling with the blessed Word
To make it yield the sense of the Lord,
That he might build a storm-proof creed
To fold the flock in at their need.

At last he builded a perfect faith,
Fenced round about with *The Lord thus saith*;
To himself he fitted the doorway's size,
Meted the light to the need of his eyes,
And knew, by a sure and inward sign,
That the work of his fingers was divine.

Then Ambrose said, " All those shall die
The eternal death who believe not as I ; "
And some were boiled, some burned in fire,
Some sawn in twain, that his heart's desire,
For the good of men's souls, might be satisfied
By the drawing of all to the righteous side.

One day, as Ambrose was seeking the truth
In his lonely walk, he saw a youth
Resting himself in the shade of a tree ;
It had never been granted him to see
So shining a face, and the good man thought
'T were pity he should not believe as he ought.

So he set himself by the young man's side,
And the state of his soul with questions tried ;
But the heart of the stranger was hardened indeed,
Nor received the stamp of the one true creed ;
And the spirit of Ambrose waxed sore to find
Such features the porch of so narrow a mind.

" As each beholds in cloud and fire
The shape that answers his own desire,
So each," said the youth, " in the Law shall find
The figure and fashion of his mind ;

And to each in his mercy hath God allowed
His several pillar of fire and cloud."

The soul of Ambrose burned with zeal
And holy wrath for the young man's weal:
" Believest thou then, most wretched youth,"
Cried he, " a dividual essence in Truth?
I fear me thy heart is too cramped with sin
To take the Lord in His glory in."

Now there bubbled beside them where they stood
A fountain of waters sweet and good;
The youth to the streamlet's brink drew near
Saying, " Ambrose, thou maker of creeds, look
        here!"
Six vases of crystal then he took,
And set them along the edge of the brook.

" As into these vessels the water I pour,
There shall one hold less, another more,
And the water unchanged, in every case,
Shall put on the figure of the vase;
O thou, who wouldst unity make through strife,
Canst thou fit this sign to the Water of Life?"

When Ambrose looked up, he stood alone,
The youth and the stream and the vases were
        gone;
But he knew, by a sense of humbled grace,
He had talked with an angel face to face,
And felt his heart change inwardly,
As he fell on his knees beneath the tree.

Felt his heart change inwardly

ABOVE AND BELOW

I

O DWELLERS in the valley-land,
  Who in deep twilight grope and cower,
Till the slow mountain's dial-hand
  Shorten to noon's triumphal hour,
While ye sit idle, do ye think
  The Lord's great work sits idle too?
That light dare not o'erleap the brink
  Of morn, because 't is dark with you?

Though yet your valleys skulk in night,
  In God's ripe fields the day is cried,
And reapers, with their sickles bright,
  Troop, singing, down the mountain-side:
Come up, and feel what health there is
  In the frank Dawn's delighted eyes,
As, bending with a pitying kiss,
  The night-shed tears of Earth she dries!

The Lord wants reapers: oh, mount up,
  Before night comes, and says, " Too late! "
Stay not for taking scrip or cup,
  The Master hungers while ye wait;
'T is from these heights alone your eyes
  The advancing spears of day can see,
That o'er the eastern hilltops rise,
  To break your long captivity.

II

Lone watcher on the mountain-height,
　It is right precious to behold
The first long surf of climbing light
　Flood all the thirsty east with gold;
But we, who in the shadow sit,
　Know also when the day is nigh,
Seeing thy shining forehead lit
　With his inspiring prophecy.

Thou hast thine office; we have ours;
　God lacks not early service here,
But what are thine eleventh hours
　He counts with us for morning cheer;
Our day, for Him, is long enough,
　And when He giveth work to do,
The bruisèd reed is amply tough
　To pierce the shield of error through.

But not the less do thou aspire
　Light's earlier messages to preach;
Keep back no syllable of fire,
　Plunge deep the rowels of thy speech.
Yet God deems not thy aeried sight
　More worthy than our twilight dim;
For meek Obedience, too, is Light,
　And following that is finding Him.

THE CAPTIVE

I⊤ was past the hour of trysting,
  But she lingered for him still;
Like a child, the eager streamlet
  Leaped and laughed adown the hill,
Happy to be free at twilight
  From its toiling at the mill.

Then the great moon on a sudden
  Ominous, and red as blood,
Startling as a new creation,
  O'er the eastern hilltop stood,
Casting deep and deeper shadows
  Through the mystery of the wood.

Dread closed vast and vague about her,
  And her thoughts turned fearfully
To her heart, if there some shelter
  From the silence there might be,
Like bare cedars leaning inland
  From the blighting of the sea.

Yet he came not, and the stillness
  Dampened round her like a tomb;
She could feel cold eyes of spirits
  Looking on her through the gloom,
She could hear the groping footsteps
  Of some blind, gigantic doom.

Suddenly the silence wavered
  Like a light mist in the wind,
For a voice broke gently through it,
  Felt like sunshine by the blind,
And the dread, like mist in sunshine,
  Furled serenely from her mind.

" Once my love, my love forever,
  Flesh or spirit, still the same,
If I failed at time of trysting,
  Deem thou not my faith to blame;
I, alas, was made a captive,
  As from Holy Land I came.

" On a green spot in the desert,
  Gleaming like an emerald star,
Where a palm-tree, in lone silence,
  Yearning for its mate afar,
Droops above a silver runnel,
  Slender as a scimitar,

" There thou 'lt find the humble postern
  To the castle of my foe;
If thy love burn clear and faithful,
  Strike the gateway, green and low,
Ask to enter, and the warder
  Surely will not say thee no."

Slept again the aspen silence,
  But her loneliness was o'er;
Round her soul a motherly patience
  Clasped its arms forevermore;

From her heart ebbed back the sorrow,
  Leaving smooth the golden shore.

Donned she now the pilgrim scallop,
  Took the pilgrim staff in hand;
Like a cloud-shade, flitting eastward,
  Wandered she o'er sea and land;
And her footsteps in the desert
  Fell like cool rain on the sand.

Soon, beneath the palm-tree's shadow,
  Knelt she at the postern low;
And thereat she knocked full gently,
  Fearing much the warder's no;
All her heart stood still and listened,
  As the door swung backward slow.

There she saw no surly warder
  With an eye like bolt and bar;
Through her soul a sense of music
  Throbbed, and, like a guardian Lar,
On the threshold stood an angel,
  Bright and silent as a star.

Fairest seemed he of God's seraphs,
  And her spirit, lily-wise,
Opened when he turned upon her
  The deep welcome of his eyes,
Sending upward to that sunlight
  All its dew for sacrifice.

Then she heard a voice come onward
    Singing with a rapture new,
As Eve heard the songs in Eden,
    Dropping earthward with the dew;
Well she knew the happy singer,
    Well the happy song she knew.

Forward leaped she o'er the threshold,
    Eager as a glancing surf;
Fell from her the spirit's languor,
    Fell from her the body's scurf;
'Neath the palm next day some Arabs
    Found a corpse upon the turf.

THE BIRCH–TREE

RIPPLING through thy branches goes the sunshine,
Among thy leaves that palpitate forever;
Ovid in thee a pining Nymph had prisoned,
The soul once of some tremulous inland river,
Quivering to tell her woe, but, ah! dumb, dumb for-
        ever!

While all the forest, witched with slumberous moon-
        shine,
Holds up its leaves in happy, happy stillness,
Waiting the dew, with breath and pulse suspended,
I hear afar thy whispering, gleamy islands,
And track thee wakeful still amid the wide-hung
        silence.

On the brink of some wood-nestled lakelet,
Thy foliage, like the tresses of a Dryad,
Dripping round thy slim white stem, whose shadow
Slopes quivering down the water's dusky quiet,
Thou shrink'st as on her bath's edge would some
        startled Naiad.

Thou art the go-between of rustic lovers;
Thy white bark has their secrets in its keeping;
Reuben writes here the happy name of Patience,
And thy lithe boughs hang murmuring and weeping
Above her, as she steals the mystery from thy keeping.

Thou art to me like my belovëd maiden,
So frankly coy, so full of trembly confidences;
Thy shadow scarce seems shade, thy pattering leaflets
Sprinkle their gathered sunshine o'er my senses,
And Nature gives me all her summer confidences.

Whether my heart with hope or sorrow tremble,
Thou sympathizest still; wild and unquiet,
I fling me down; thy ripple, like a river,
Flows valleyward, where calmness is, and by it
My heart is floated down into the land of quiet.

AN INTERVIEW WITH MILES STANDISH

I sat one evening in my room,
    In that sweet hour of twilight
When blended thoughts, half light, half gloom,
    Throng through the spirit's skylight;

The flames by fits curled round the bars,
  Or up the chimney crinkled,
While embers dropped like falling stars,
  And in the ashes tinkled.

I sat and mused; the fire burned low,
  And o'er my senses stealing,
Crept something of the ruddy glow
  That bloomed on wall and ceiling;
My pictures (they are very few,
  The heads of ancient wise men)
Smoothed down their knotted fronts, and grew
  As rosy as excisemen.

My antique high-backed Spanish chair
  Felt thrills through wood and leather,
That had been strangers since whilere,
  'Mid Andalusian heather,
The oak that built its sturdy frame
  His happy arms stretched over
The ox whose fortunate hide became
  The bottom's polished cover.

It came out in that famous bark,
  That brought our sires intrepid,
Capacious as another ark
  For furniture decrepit;
For, as that saved of bird and beast
  A pair for propagation,
So has the seed of these increased
  And furnished half the nation.

Kings sit, they say, in slippery seats;
   But those slant precipices
Of ice the northern voyager meets
   Less slippery are than this is;
To cling therein would pass the wit
   Of royal man or woman,
And whatsoe'er can stay in it
   Is more or less than human.

I offer to all bores this perch,
   Dear well-intentioned people
With heads as void as week-day church,
   Tongues longer than the steeple;
To folks with missions, whose gaunt eyes
   See golden ages rising, —
Salt of the earth! in what queer Guys
   Thou 'rt fond of crystallizing!

My wonder, then, was not unmixed
   With merciful suggestion,
When, as my roving eyes grew fixed
   Upon the chair in question,
I saw its trembling arms enclose
   A figure grim and rusty,
Whose doublet plain and plainer hose
   Were something worn and dusty.

Now even such men as Nature forms
   Merely to fill the street with,
Once turned to ghost by hungry worms,
   Are serious things to meet with;

Your penitent spirits are no jokes,
   And, though I 'm not averse to
A quiet shade, even they are folks
   One cares not to speak first to.

Who knows, thought I, but he has come,
   By Charon kindly ferried,
To tell me of a mighty sum
   Behind my wainscot buried?
There is a buccaneerish air
   About that garb outlandish —
Just then the ghost drew up his chair
   And said, " My name is Standish.

" I come from Plymouth, deadly bored
   With toasts, and songs, and speeches,
As long and flat as my old sword,
   As threadbare as my breeches:
They understand us Pilgrims! they,
   Smooth men with rosy faces,
Strength's knots and gnarls all pared away,
   And varnish in their places!

" We had some toughness in our grain,
   The eye to rightly see us is
Not just the one that lights the brain
   Of drawing-room Tyrtæuses:
They talk about their Pilgrim blood,
   Their birthright high and holy!
A mountain-stream that ends in mud
   Methinks is melancholy.

" He had stiff knees, the Puritan,
    That were not good at bending ;
The homespun dignity of man
    He thought was worth defending ;
He did not, with his pinchbeck ore,
    His country's shame forgotten,
Gild Freedom's coffin o'er and o'er,
    When all within was rotten.

" These loud ancestral boasts of yours,
    How can they else than vex us ?
Where were your dinner orators
    When Slavery grasped at Texas ?
Dumb on his knees was every one
    That now is bold as Cæsar ;
Mere pegs to hang an office on
    Such stalwart men as these are."

" Good sir," I said, " you seem much stirred ;
    The sacred compromises — "
" Now God confound the dastard word !
    My gall thereat arises :
Northward it hath this sense alone,
    That you, your conscience blinding,
Shall bow your fool's nose to the stone,
    When Slavery feels like grinding.

" 'T is shame to see such painted sticks
    In Vane's and Winthrop's places,
To see your spirit of Seventy-six
    Drag humbly in the traces,
    I

With Slavery's lash upon her back,
  And herds of office-holders
To shout applause, as, with a crack,
  It peels her patient shoulders.

" *We* forefathers to such a rout ! —
  No, by my faith in God's word ! "
Half rose the ghost, and half drew out
  The ghost of his old broadsword,
Then thrust it slowly back again,
  And said, with reverent gesture,
" No, Freedom, no ! blood should not stain
  The hem of thy white vesture.

" I feel the soul in me draw near
  The mount of prophesying ;
In this bleak wilderness I hear
  A John the Baptist crying ;
Far in the east I see upleap
  The streaks of first forewarning,
And they who sowed the light shall reap
  The golden sheaves of morning.

" Child of our travail and our woe,
  Light in our day of sorrow,
Through my rapt spirit I foreknow
  The glory of thy morrow ;
I hear great steps, that through the shade
  Draw nigher still and nigher,
And voices call like that which bade
  The prophet come up higher."

I looked, no form mine eyes could find,
    I heard the red cock crowing,
And through my window-chinks the wind
    A dismal tune was blowing;
Thought I, My neighbor Buckingham
    Hath somewhat in him gritty,
Some Pilgrim-stuff that hates all sham,
    And he will print my ditty.

ON THE CAPTURE OF FUGITIVE SLAVES
NEAR WASHINGTON

Look on who will in apathy, and stifle they who
    can,
The sympathies, the hopes, the words, that make man
    truly man;
Let those whose hearts are dungeoned up with inter-
    est or with ease
Consent to hear with quiet pulse of loathsome deeds
    like these!

I first drew in New England's air, and from her hardy
    breast
Sucked in the tyrant-hating milk that will not let me
    rest;
And if my words seem treason to the dullard and the
    tame,
'T is but my Bay-State dialect, — our fathers spake
    the same!

Shame on the costly mockery of piling stone on stone
To those who won our liberty, the heroes dead and
    gone,
While we look coldly on and see law-shielded ruffians
    slay
The men who fain would win their own, the heroes
    of to-day!

Are we pledged to craven silence? Oh, fling it to the
    wind,
The parchment wall that bars us from the least of
    human kind,
That makes us cringe and temporize, and dumbly
    stand at rest,
While Pity's burning flood of words is red-hot in the
    breast!

Though we break our fathers' promise, we have
    nobler duties first;
The traitor to Humanity is the traitor most accursed;
Man is more than Constitutions; better rot beneath
    the sod,
Than be true to Church and State while we are
    doubly false to God!

We owe allegiance to the State; but deeper, truer,
    more,
To the sympathies that God hath set within our
    spirit's core;
Our country claims our fealty; we grant it so, but then
Before Man made us citizens, great Nature made us
    men.

He's true to God who's true to man; wherever
    wrong is done,
To the humblest and the weakest, 'neath the all-
    beholding sun,
That wrong is also done to us; and they are slaves
    most base,
Whose love of right is for themselves, and not for all
    their race.

God works for all. Ye cannot hem the hope of
    being free
With parallels of latitude, with mountain-range or sea.
Put golden padlocks on Truth's lips, be callous as ye
    will,
From soul to soul, o'er all the world, leaps one elec-
    tric thrill.

Chain down your slaves with ignorance, ye cannot
    keep apart,
With all your craft of tyranny, the human heart from
    heart :
When first the Pilgrims landed on the Bay State's iron
    shore,
The word went forth that slavery should one day be
    no more.

Out from the land of bondage 't is decreed our slaves
    shall go,
And signs to us are offered, as erst to Pharaoh;
If we are blind, their exodus, like Israel's of yore,
Through a Red Sea is doomed to be, whose surges are
    of gore.

'T is ours to save our brethren, with peace and love
      to win
Their darkened hearts from error, ere they harden it
      to sin ;
But if before his duty man with listless spirit stands,
Ere long the Great Avenger takes the work from out
      his hands.

TO THE DANDELION

DEAR common flower, that grow'st beside the way,
Fringing the dusty road with harmless gold,
    First pledge of blithesome May,
Which children pluck, and full of pride uphold,
  High-hearted buccaneers, o'erjoyed that they
An Eldorado in the grass have found,
    Which not the rich earth's ample round
    May match in wealth, thou art more dear to me
    Than all the prouder summer-blooms may be.

Gold such as thine ne'er drew the Spanish prow
Through the primæval hush of Indian seas,
    Nor wrinkled the lean brow
Of age, to rob the lover's heart of ease ;
  'T is the Spring's largess, which she scatters now
To rich and poor alike, with lavish hand,
    Though most hearts never understand
    To take it at God's value, but pass by
    The offered wealth with unrewarded eye.

Thou art my tropics and mine Italy;
To look at thee unlocks a warmer clime;
    The eyes thou givest me
Are in the heart, and heed not space or time:
    Not in mid June the golden-cuirassed bee
Feels a more summer-like warm ravishment
    In the white lily's breezy tent,
    His fragrant Sybaris, than I, when first
    From the dark green thy yellow circles burst.

Then think I of deep shadows on the grass,
Of meadows where in sun the cattle graze,
    Where, as the breezes pass,
The gleaming rushes lean a thousand ways,
    Of leaves that slumber in a cloudy mass,
Or whiten in the wind, of waters blue
    That from the distance sparkle through
    Some woodland gap, and of a sky above,
    Where one white cloud like a stray lamb doth
      move.

My childhood's earliest thoughts are linked with
      thee;
The sight of thee calls back the robin's song,
    Who, from the dark old tree
Beside the door, sang clearly all day long,
    And I, secure in childish piety,
Listened as if I heard an angel sing
    With news from heaven, which he could bring
    Fresh every day to my untainted ears
    When birds and flowers and I were happy peers.

How like a prodigal doth Nature seem,
When thou, for all thy gold, so common art!
    Thou teachest me to deem
More sacredly of every human heart,
    Since each reflects in joy its scanty gleam
Of heaven, and could some wondrous secret show,
        Did we but pay the love we owe,
    And with a child's undoubting wisdom look
    On all these living pages of God's book.

THE GHOST–SEER

Ye who, passing graves by night,
Glance not to the left or right,
Lest a spirit should arise,
Cold and white, to freeze your eyes,
Some weak phantom, which your doubt
Shapes upon the dark without
From the dark within, a guess
At the spirit's deathlessness,
Which ye entertain with fear
In your self-built dungeon here,
Where ye sell your God-given lives
Just for gold to buy you gyves, —
Ye without a shudder meet
In the city's noonday street,
Spirits sadder and more dread
Than from out the clay have fled,
Buried, beyond hope of light,
In the body's haunted night!

See ye not that woman pale?
There are bloodhounds on her trail!
Bloodhounds two, all gaunt and lean
(For the soul their scent is keen),
Want and Sin, and Sin is last,
They have followed far and fast;
Want gave tongue, and, at her howl,
Sin awakened with a growl.
Ah, poor girl! she had a right
To a blessing from the light;
Title-deeds to sky and earth
God gave to her at her birth;
But, before they were enjoyed,
Poverty had made them void,
And had drunk the sunshine up
From all Nature's ample cup,
Leaving her a first-born's share
In the dregs of darkness there.
Often, on the sidewalk bleak,
Hungry, all alone, and weak,
She has seen, in night and storm,
Rooms o'erflow with firelight warm,
Which, outside the window-glass,
Doubled all the cold, alas!
Till each ray that on her fell
Stabbed her like an icicle,
And she almost loved the wail
Of the bloodhounds on her trail.
Till the floor becomes her bier,
She shall feel their pantings near,
Close upon her very heels,
Spite of all the din of wheels;

Shivering on her pallet poor,
She shall hear them at the door
Whine and scratch to be let in,
Sister bloodhounds, Want and Sin!

Hark! that rustle of a dress,
Stiff with lavish costliness!
Here comes one whose cheek would
    flush
But to have her garment brush
'Gainst the girl whose fingers thin
Wove the weary broidery in,
Bending backward from her toil,
Lest her tears the silk might soil,
And, in midnights chill and mirk,
Stitched her life into the work,
Shaping from her bitter thought
Heart's-ease and forget-me-not,
Satirizing her despair
With the emblems woven there.
Little doth the wearer heed
Of the heart-break in the brede;
A hyena by her side
Skulks, down-looking,—it is Pride.
He digs for her in the earth,
Where lie all her claims of birth,
With his foul paws rooting o'er
Some long-buried ancestor,
Who, perhaps, a statue won,
By the ill deeds he had done,
By the innocent blood he shed,
By the desolation spread

Over happy villages,
Blotting out the smile of peace.
There walks Judas, he who sold
Yesterday his Lord for gold,
Sold God's presence in his heart
For a proud step in the mart;
He hath dealt in flesh and blood;
At the bank his name is good;
At the bank, and only there,
'T is a marketable ware.
In his eyes that stealthy gleam
Was not learned of sky or stream,
But it has the cold, hard glint
Of new dollars from the mint.
Open now your spirit's eyes,
Look through that poor clay disguise
Which has thickened, day by day,
Till it keeps all light at bay,
And his soul in pitchy gloom
Gropes about its narrow tomb,
From whose dank and slimy walls
Drop by drop the horror falls.
Look! a serpent lank and cold
Hugs his spirit fold on fold;
From his heart, all day and night,
It doth suck God's blessed light.
Drink it will, and drink it must,
Till the cup holds naught but dust;
All day long he hears it hiss,
Writhing in its fiendish bliss;
All night long he sees its eyes
Flicker with foul ecstasies,

As the spirit ebbs away
Into the absorbing clay.
Who is he that skulks, afraid
Of the trust he has betrayed,
Shuddering if perchance a gleam
Of old nobleness should stream
Through the pent, unwholesome room,
Where his shrunk soul cowers in gloom,
Spirit sad beyond the rest
By more instinct for the best?
'T is a poet who was sent
For a bad world's punishment,
By compelling it to see
Golden glimpses of To Be,
By compelling it to hear
Songs that prove the angels near;
Who was sent to be the tongue
Of the weak and spirit-wrung,
Whence the fiery-winged Despair
In men's shrinking eyes might flare.
'T is our hope doth fashion us
To base use or glorious:
He who might have been a lark
Of Truth's morning, from the dark
Raining down melodious hope
Of a freer, broader scope,
Aspirations, prophecies,
Of the spirit's full sunrise,
Chose to be a bird of night,
That, with eyes refusing light,
Hooted from some hollow tree
Of the world's idolatry.

'T is his punishment to hear
Sweep of eager pinions near,
And his own vain wings to feel
Drooping downward to his heel,
All their grace and import lost,
Burdening his weary ghost :
Ever walking by his side
He must see his angel guide,
Who at intervals doth turn
Looks on him so sadly stern,
With such ever-new surprise
Of hushed anguish in her eyes,
That it seems the light of day
From around him shrinks away,
Or drops blunted from the wall
Built around him by his fall.
Then the mountains, whose white peaks
Catch the morning's earliest streaks,
He must see, where prophets sit,
Turning east their faces lit,
Whence, with footsteps beautiful,
To the earth, yet dim and dull,
They the gladsome tidings bring
Of the sunlight's hastening :
Never can these hills of bliss
Be o'erclimbed by feet like his !

But enough ! Oh, do not dare
From the next the veil to tear,
Woven of station, trade, or dress,
More obscene than nakedness,
Wherewith plausible culture drapes

Fallen Nature's myriad shapes!
Let us rather love to mark
How the unextinguished spark
Still gleams through the thin disguise
Of our customs, pomps, and lies,
And, not seldom blown to flame,
Vindicates its ancient claim.

STUDIES FOR TWO HEADS

I

SOME sort of heart I know is hers, —
  I chanced to feel her pulse one night ;
A brain she has that never errs,
  And yet is never nobly right ;
It does not leap to great results,
  But, in some corner out of sight,
  Suspects a spot of latent blight,
  And, o'er the impatient infinite,
She bargains, haggles, and consults.

Her eye, — it seems a chemic test
  And drops upon you like an acid ;
It bites you with unconscious zest,
  So clear and bright, so coldly placid ;
It holds you quietly aloof,
  It holds, — and yet it does not win you ;
It merely puts you to the proof
  And sorts what qualities are in you ;
It smiles, but never brings you nearer,

It lights, — her nature draws not nigh ;
'T is but that yours is growing clearer
   To her assays ; — yes, try and try,
   You 'll get no deeper than her eye.

There, you are classified: she 's gone
   Far, far away into her self ;
Each with its Latin label on,
Your poor components, one by one,
   Are laid upon their proper shelf
In her compact and ordered mind,
And what of you is left behind
Is no more to her than the wind ;
In that clear brain, which, day and night,
   No movement of the heart e'er jostles,
Her friends are ranged on left and right, —
Here, silex, hornblende, sienite ;
   There, animal remains and fossils.

And yet, O subtile analyst,
   That canst each property detect
Of mood or grain, that canst untwist
   Each tangled skein of intellect,
And with thy scalpel eyes lay bare
Each mental nerve more fine than air, —
   O brain exact, that in thy scales
Canst weigh the sun and never err,
   For once thy patient science fails,
   One problem still defies thy art ; —
Thou never canst compute for her
The distance and diameter
   Of any simple human heart.

II

Hear him but speak, and you will feel
  The shadows of the portico
Over your tranquil spirit steal,
    To modulate all joy and woe
    To one subdued, subduing glow;
Above our squabbling business-hours,
Like Phidian Jove's, his beauty lowers,
His nature satirizes ours;
    A form and front of Attic grace,
    He shames the higgling market-place,
And dwarfs our more mechanic powers.

What throbbing verse can fitly render
That face so pure, so trembling-tender?
  Sensation glimmers through its rest,
It speaks unmanacled by words,
  As full of motion as a nest
That palpitates with unfledged birds;
  'T is likest to Bethesda's stream,
Forewarned through all its thrilling springs,
  White with the angel's coming gleam,
And rippled with his fanning wings.

Hear him unfold his plots and plans,
And larger destinies seem man's;
You conjure from his glowing face
The omen of a fairer race;
With one grand trope he boldly spans
  The gulf wherein so many fall,
  'Twixt possible and actual;

His first swift word, talaria-shod,
Exuberant with conscious God,
Out of the choir of planets blots
The present earth with all its spots.

Himself unshaken as the sky,
His words, like whirlwinds, spin on high
    Systems and creeds pellmell together;
'T is strange as to a deaf man's eye,
While trees uprooted splinter by,
    The dumb turmoil of stormy weather;
    Less of iconoclast than shaper,
His spirit, safe behind the reach
Of the tornado of his speech,
    Burns calmly as a glowworm's taper.

So great in speech, but, ah! in act
    So overrun with vermin troubles,
The coarse, sharp-cornered, ugly fact
    Of life collapses all his bubbles:
Had he but lived in Plato's day,
    He might, unless my fancy errs,
Have shared that golden voice's sway
    O'er barefooted philosophers.
Our nipping climate hardly suits
The ripening of ideal fruits:
His theories vanquish us all summer,
But winter makes him dumb and dumber;
To see him mid life's needful things
    Is something painfully bewildering;
He seems an angel with clipt wings
    Tied to a mortal wife and children,

I

And by a brother seraph taken
In the act of eating eggs and bacon.
Like a clear fountain, his desire
  Exults and leaps toward the light,
In every drop it says " Aspire ! "
  Striving for more ideal height ;
And as the fountain, falling thence,
  Crawls baffled through the common gutter,
So, from his speech's eminence,
He shrinks into the present tense,
  Unkinged by foolish bread and butter.

Yet smile not, worldling, for in deeds
  Not all of life that 's brave and wise is ;
He strews an ampler future's seeds,
  'T is your fault if no harvest rises ;
Smooth back the sneer ; for is it naught
  That all he is and has is Beauty's ?
By soul the soul's gains must be wrought,
The Actual claims our coarser thought,
  The Ideal hath its higher duties.

ON A PORTRAIT OF DANTE BY GIOTTO

Can this be thou who, lean and pale,
  With such immitigable eye
Didst look upon those writhing souls in bale,
  And note each vengeance, and pass by
Unmoved, save when thy heart by chance
Cast backward one forbidden glance,

And saw Francesca, with child's glee,
Subdue and mount thy wild-horse knee
And with proud hands control its fiery prance?

With half-drooped lids, and smooth, round brow,
    And eye remote, that inly sees
Fair Beatrice's spirit wandering now
    In some sea-lulled Hesperides,
Thou movest through the jarring street,
Secluded from the noise of feet
    By her gift-blossom in thy hand,
    Thy branch of palm from Holy Land; —
No trace is here of ruin's fiery sleet.

Yet there is something round thy lips
    That prophesies the coming doom,
The soft, gray herald-shadow ere the eclipse
    Notches the perfect disk with gloom;
A something that would banish thee,
And thine untamed pursuer be,
    From men and their unworthy fates,
    Though Florence had not shut her gates,
And Grief had loosed her clutch and let thee free.

Ah! he who follows fearlessly
    The beckonings of a poet-heart
Shall wander, and without the world's decree,
    A banished man in field and mart;
Harder than Florence' walls the bar
Which with deaf sternness holds him far
    From home and friends, till death's release,
    And makes his only prayer for peace,
Like thine, scarred veteran of a lifelong war!

ON THE DEATH OF A FRIEND'S CHILD

DEATH never came so nigh to me before,
Nor showed me his mild face : oft had I mused
Of calm and peace and safe forgetfulness,
Of folded hands, closed eyes, and heart at rest,
And slumber sound beneath a flowery turf,
Of faults forgotten, and an inner place
Kept sacred for us in the heart of friends ;
But these were idle fancies, satisfied
With the mere husk of this great mystery,
And dwelling in the outward shows of things.
Heaven is not mounted to on wings of dreams,
Nor doth the unthankful happiness of youth
Aim thitherward, but floats from bloom to bloom,
With earth's warm patch of sunshine well content :
'T is sorrow builds the shining ladder up,
Whose golden rounds are our calamities,
Whereon our firm feet planting, nearer God
The spirit climbs, and hath its eyes unsealed.

True is it that Death's face seems stern and cold,
When he is sent to summon those we love,
But all God's angels come to us disguised ;
Sorrow and sickness, poverty and death,
One after other lift their frowning masks,
And we behold the seraph's face beneath,
All radiant with the glory and the calm
Of having looked upon the front of God.

With every anguish of our earthly part
The spirit's sight grows clearer; this was meant
When Jesus touched the blind man's lids with clay.
Life is the jailer, Death the angel sent
To draw the unwilling bolts and set us free.
He flings not ope the ivory gate of Rest, —
Only the fallen spirit knocks at that, —
But to benigner regions beckons us,
To destinies of more rewarded toil.
In the hushed chamber, sitting by the dead,
It grates on us to hear the flood of life
Whirl rustling onward, senseless of our loss.
The bee hums on; around the blossomed vine
Whirs the light humming-bird; the cricket chirps;
The locust's shrill alarum stings the ear;
Hard by, the cock shouts lustily; from farm to farm,
His cheery brothers, telling of the sun,
Answer, till far away the joyance dies:
We never knew before how God had filled
The summer air with happy living sounds;
All round us seems an overplus of life,
And yet the one dear heart lies cold and still.
It is most strange, when the great miracle
Hath for our sakes been done, when we have had
Our inwardest experience of God,
When with His presence still the room expands,
And is awed after Him, that naught is changed,
That Nature's face looks unacknowledging,
And the mad world still dances heedless on
After its butterflies, and gives no sign.
'T is hard at first to see it all aright:
In vain Faith blows her trump to summon back

Her scattered troop: yet, through the clouded
    glass
Of our own bitter tears, we learn to look
Undazzled on the kindness of God's face;
Earth is too dark, and Heaven alone shines through.

It is no little thing, when a fresh soul
And a fresh heart, with their unmeasured scope
For good, not gravitating earthward yet,
But circling in diviner periods,
Are sent into the world, — no little thing,
When this unbounded possibility
Into the outer silence is withdrawn.
Ah, in this world, where every guiding thread
Ends suddenly in the one sure centre, death,
The visionary hand of Might-have-been
Alone can fill Desire's cup to the brim!

How changed, dear friend, are thy part and thy
    child's!
He bends above *thy* cradle now, or holds
His warning finger out to be thy guide;
Thou art the nursling now; he watches thee
Slow learning, one by one, the secret things
Which are to him used sights of every day;
He smiles to see thy wondering glances con
The grass and pebbles of the spirit-world,
To thee miraculous; and he will teach
Thy knees their due observances of prayer.
Children are God's apostles, day by day
Sent forth to preach of love, and hope, and
    peace;

Nor hath thy babe his mission left undone.
To me, at least, his going hence hath given
Serener thoughts and nearer to the skies,
And opened a new fountain in my heart
For thee, my friend, and all: and oh, if Death
More near approaches meditates, and clasps
Even now some dearer, more reluctant hand,
God, strengthen thou my faith, that I may see
That 't is thine angel, who, with loving haste,
Unto the service of the inner shrine,
Doth waken thy belovëd with a kiss.

EURYDICE

HEAVEN's cup held down to me I drain,
The sunshine mounts and spurs my brain;
Bathing in grass, with thirsty eye
I suck the last drop of the sky;
With each hot sense I draw to the lees
The quickening outdoor influences,
And empty to each radiant comer
A supernaculum of summer.
Not, Bacchus, all thy grosser juice
Could bring enchantment so profuse,
Though for its press each grape-bunch had
The white feet of an Oread.

Through our coarse art gleam, now and then,
The features of angelic men:
'Neath the lewd Satyr's veiling paint

Glows forth the Sibyl, Muse, or Saint;
The dauber's botch no more obscures
The mighty master's portraitures.
And who can say what luckier beam
The hidden glory shall redeem,
For what chance clod the soul may wait
To stumble on its nobler fate,
Or why, to his unwarned abode,
Still by surprises comes the God?
Some moment, nailed on sorrow's cross,
May mediate a whole youth's loss,
Some windfall joy, we know not whence,
Redeem a lifetime's rash expense,
And, suddenly wise, the soul may mark,
Stripped of their simulated dark,
Mountains of gold that pierce the sky,
Girdling its valleyed poverty.

I feel ye, childhood's hopes, return,
With olden heats my pulses burn, —
Mine be the self-forgetting sweep,
The torrent impulse swift and wild,
Wherewith Taghkanic's rockborn child
Dares gloriously the dangerous leap,
And, in his sky-descended mood,
Transmutes each drop of sluggish blood,
By touch of bravery's simple wand,
To amethyst and diamond,
Proving himself no bastard slip,
But the true granite-cradled one,
Nursed with the rock's primæval drip,
The cloud-embracing mountain's son!

Prayer breathed in vain ! no wish's sway
Rebuilds the vanished yesterday;
For plated wares of Sheffield stamp
We gave the old Aladdin's lamp;
'T is we are changed; ah, whither went
That undesigned abandonment,
That wise, unquestioning content,
Which could erect its microcosm
Out of a weed's neglected blossom,
Could call up Arthur and his peers
By a low moss's clump of spears,
Or, in its shingle trireme launched,
Where Charles in some green inlet branched,
Could venture for the golden fleece
And dragon-watched Hesperides,
Or, from its ripple-shattered fate,
Ulysses' chances re-create?
When, heralding life's every phase,
There glowed a goddess-veiling haze,
A plenteous, forewarning grace,
Like that more tender dawn that flies
Before the full moon's ample rise?
Methinks thy parting glory shines
Through yonder grove of singing pines;
At that elm-vista's end I trace
Dimly thy sad leave-taking face,
Eurydice ! Eurydice !
The tremulous leaves repeat to me
Eurydice ! Eurydice !
No gloomier Orcus swallows thee
Than the unclouded sunset's glow;
Thine is at least Elysian woe;

Thou hast Good's natural decay,
And fadest like a star away
Into an atmosphere whose shine
With fuller day o'ermasters thine,
Entering defeat as 't were a shrine;
For us, — we turn life's diary o'er
To find but one word, — Nevermore.

SHE CAME AND WENT

As a twig trembles, which a bird
    Lights on to sing, then leaves unbent,
So is my memory thrilled and stirred; —
    I only know she came and went.

As clasps some lake, by gusts unriven,
    The blue dome's measureless content,
So my soul held that moment's heaven; —
    I only know she came and went.

As, at one bound, our swift spring heaps
    The orchards full of bloom and scent,
So clove her May my wintry sleeps; —
    I only know she came and went.

An angel stood and met my gaze,
    Through the low doorway of my tent;
The tent is struck, the vision stays; —
    I only know she came and went.

Oh, when the room grows slowly dim,
　And life's last oil is nearly spent,
One gush of light these eyes will brim,
　Only to think she came and went.

THE CHANGELING

I HAD a little daughter,
　And she was given to me
To lead me gently backward
　To the Heavenly Father's knee,
That I, by the force of nature,
　Might in some dim wise divine
The depth of his infinite patience
　To this wayward soul of mine.

I know not how others saw her,
　But to me she was wholly fair,
And the light of the heaven she came from
　Still lingered and gleamed in her hair;
For it was as wavy and golden,
　And as many changes took,
As the shadows of sun-gilt ripples
　On the yellow bed of a brook.

To what can I liken her smiling
　Upon me, her kneeling lover,
How it leaped from her lips to her eyelids,
　And dimpled her wholly over,
Till her outstretched hands smiled also,
　And I almost seemed to see

The very heart of her mother
  Sending sun through her veins to me!

She had been with us scarce a twelvemonth,
  And it hardly seemed a day,
When a troop of wandering angels
  Stole my little daughter away;
Or perhaps those heavenly Zingari
  But loosed the hampering strings,
And when they had opened her cage-door,
  My little bird used her wings.

But they left in her stead a changeling,
  A little angel child,
That seems like her bud in full blossom,
  And smiles as she never smiled:
When I wake in the morning, I see it
  Where she always used to lie,
And I feel as weak as a violet
  Alone 'neath the awful sky.

As weak, yet as trustful also;
  For the whole year long I see
All the wonders of faithful Nature
  Still worked for the love of me;
Winds wander, and dews drip earthward,
  Rain falls, suns rise and set,
Earth whirls, and all but to prosper
  A poor little violet.

This child is not mine as the first was,
  I cannot sing it to rest,

I cannot lift it up fatherly
   And bliss it upon my breast;
Yet it lies in my little one's cradle
   And sits in my little one's chair,
And the light of the heaven she's gone to
   Transfigures its golden hair.

THE PIONEER

WHAT man would live coffined with brick and
    stone,
  Imprisoned from the healing touch of air,
  And cramped with selfish landmarks everywhere,
When all before him stretches, furrowless and lone,
  The unmapped prairie none can fence or own?

What man would read and read the selfsame
    faces,
  And, like the marbles which the windmill grinds,
  Rub smooth forever with the same smooth minds,
This year retracing last year's, every year's, dull
    traces,
  When there are woods and un-penfolded spaces?

What man o'er one old thought would pore and
    pore,
  Shut like a book between its covers thin
  For every fool to leave his dog's-ears in,
When solitude is his, and God forevermore,
  Just for the opening of a paltry door?

What man would watch life's oozy element
   Creep Letheward forever, when he might
   Down some great river drift beyond men's sight,
To where the undethronëd forest's royal tent
   Broods with its hush o'er half a continent?

What man with men would push and altercate,
   Piecing out crooked means to crooked ends,
   When he can have the skies and woods for
      friends,
Snatch back the rudder of his undismantled fate,
   And in himself be ruler, church, and state?

Cast leaves and feathers rot in last year's nest,
   The wingëd brood, flown thence, new dwellings
      plan;
   The serf of his own Past is not a man;
To change and change is life, to move and never
      rest;—
   Not what we are, but what we hope, is best.

The wild, free woods make no man halt or
      blind;
   Cities rob men of eyes and hands and feet,
   Patching one whole of many incomplete;
The general preys upon the individual mind,
   And each alone is helpless as the wind.

Each man is some man's servant; every soul
   Is by some other's presence quite discrowned;
   Each owes the next through all the imperfect
      round,

Yet not with mutual help; each man is his own
    goal,
And the whole earth must stop to pay him toll.

Here, life the undiminished man demands;
    New faculties stretch out to meet new wants;
    What Nature asks, that Nature also grants;
Here man is lord, not drudge, of eyes and feet and
    hands,
And to his life is knit with hourly bands.

Come out, then, from the old thoughts and old
    ways,
    Before you harden to a crystal cold
    Which the new life can shatter, but not mould;
Freedom for you still waits, still, looking backward,
    stays,
    But widens still the irretrievable space.

LONGING

OF all the myriad moods of mind
    That through the soul come thronging,
Which one was e'er so dear, so kind,
    So beautiful as Longing?
The thing we long for, that we are
    For one transcendent moment,
Before the Present poor and bare
    Can make its sneering comment.

Still, through our paltry stir and strife,
  Glows down the wished Ideal,
And Longing moulds in clay what Life
  Carves in the marble Real;
To let the new life in, we know,
  Desire must ope the portal;
Perhaps the longing to be so
  Helps make the soul immortal.

Longing is God's fresh heavenward will
  With our poor earthward striving;
We quench it that we may be still
  Content with merely living;
But, would we learn that heart's full scope
  Which we are hourly wronging,
Our lives must climb from hope to hope
  And realize our longing.

Ah! let us hope that to our praise
  Good God not only reckons
The moments when we tread His ways,
  But when the spirit beckons, —
That some slight good is also wrought
  Beyond self-satisfaction,
When we are simply good in thought,
  Howe'er we fail in action.

ODE TO FRANCE

FEBRUARY 1848

I

As flake by flake the beetling avalanches
  Build up their imminent crags of noiseless snow,
Till some chance thrill the loosened ruin launches
  In unwarned havoc on the roofs below,
So grew and gathered through the silent years
  The madness of a People, wrong by wrong.
There seemed no strength in the dumb toiler's
      tears,
  No strength in suffering; but the Past was strong:
The brute despair of trampled centuries
  Leaped up with one hoarse yell and snapped its
      bands,
  Groped for its right with horny, callous hands,
And stared around for God with bloodshot eyes.
  What wonder if those palms were all too hard
For nice distinctions, — if that mænad throng —
  They whose thick atmosphere no bard
Had shivered with the lightning of his song,
  Brutes with the memories and desires of men,
  Whose chronicles were writ with iron pen,
    In the crooked shoulder and the forehead low,
      Set wrong to balance wrong,
      And physicked woe with woe?

1

II

They did as they were taught; not theirs the blame,
If men who scattered firebrands reaped the flame:
　　They trampled Peace beneath their savage feet,
　　　　And by her golden tresses drew
　　Mercy along the pavement of the street.
O Freedom! Freedom! is thy morning-dew
　　　　So gory red? Alas, thy light had ne'er
　　　　Shone in upon the chaos of their lair!
They reared to thee such symbol as they knew,
　　　　And worshipped it with flame and blood,
　　　　A Vengeance, axe in hand, that stood
Holding a tyrant's head up by the clotted hair.

III

What wrongs   the   Oppressor   suffered,   these   we
　　　　know;
　　These have found piteous voice in song and prose;
But for the Oppressed, their darkness and their woe,
　　Their grinding centuries, — what Muse had those?
Though hall and palace had nor eyes nor ears,
　　Hardening a people's heart to senseless stone,
Thou   knewest   them,   O   Earth,   that   drank   their
　　　　tears,
　　O Heaven, that heard their inarticulate moan!
They noted down their fetters, link by link;
Coarse was the hand that scrawled, and red the ink;
　　Rude was their score, as suits unlettered men,
Notched with a headsman's axe upon a block:
What marvel if, when came the avenging shock,
　　'T was Atë, not Urania, held the pen?

IV

With eye averted, and an anguished frown,
    Loathingly glides the Muse through scenes of strife,
Where, like the heart of Vengeance up and down,
    Throbs in its framework the blood-muffled knife;
Slow are the steps of Freedom, but her feet
    Turn never backward: hers no bloody glare;
Her light is calm, and innocent, and sweet,
    And where it enters there is no despair:
Not first on palace and cathedral spire
Quivers and gleams that unconsuming fire;
    While these stand black against her morning skies,
The peasant sees it leap from peak to peak
    Along his hills; the craftsman's burning eyes
Own with cool tears its influence mother-meek;
    It lights the poet's heart up like a star;
    Ah! while the tyrant deemed it still afar,
And twined with golden threads his futile snare,
    That swift, convicting glow all round him ran;
        'T was close beside him there,
    Sunrise whose Memnon is the soul of man.

V

O Broker-King, is this thy wisdom's fruit?
    A dynasty plucked out as 't were a weed
    Grown rankly in a night, that leaves no seed!
Could eighteen years strike down no deeper root?
    But now thy vulture eye was turned on Spain;
A shout from Paris, and thy crown falls off,
    Thy race has ceased to reign,
And thou become a fugitive and scoff:

Slippery the feet that mount by stairs of gold,
And weakest of all fences one of steel;
Go and keep school again like him of old,
The Syracusan tyrant; — thou mayst feel
Royal amid a birch-swayed commonweal!

VI

Not long can he be ruler who allows
His time to run before him; thou wast naught
Soon as the strip of gold about thy brows
Was no more emblem of the People's thought:
Vain were thy bayonets against the foe
Thou hadst to cope with; thou didst wage
War not with Frenchmen merely; — no,
Thy strife was with the Spirit of the Age,
The invisible Spirit whose first breath divine
Scattered thy frail endeavor,
And, like poor last year's leaves, whirled thee and thine
Into the Dark forever!

VII

Is here no triumph? Nay, what though
The yellow blood of Trade meanwhile should pour
Along its arteries a shrunken flow,
And the idle canvas droop around the shore?
These do not make a state,
Nor keep it great;
I think God made
The earth for man, not trade;
And where each humblest human creature
Can stand, no more suspicious or afraid,
Erect and kingly in his right of nature,

To heaven and earth knit with harmonious ties, —
  Where I behold the exultation
  Of manhood glowing in those eyes
    That had been dark for ages,
    Or only lit with bestial loves and rages,
    There I behold a Nation :
      The France which lies
    Between the Pyrenees and Rhine
     Is the least part of France;
I see her rather in the soul whose shine
Burns through the craftsman's grimy countenance,
    In the new energy divine
     Of Toil's enfranchised glance.

VIII

    And if it be a dream,
  If the great Future be the little Past
  'Neath a new mask, which drops and shows at last
  The same weird, mocking face to balk and blast,
Yet, Muse, a gladder measure suits the theme,
    And the Tyrtæan harp
    Loves notes more resolute and sharp,
Throbbing, as throbs the bosom, hot and fast :
    Such visions are of morning,
    Theirs is no vague forewarning,
The dreams which nations dream come true,
    And shape the world anew;
      If this be a sleep,
     Make it long, make it deep,
O Father, who sendest the harvests men reap!
     While Labor so sleepeth,
     His sorrow is gone,

No longer he weepeth,
But smileth and steepeth
   His thoughts in the dawn ;
He heareth Hope yonder
   Rain, lark-like, her fancies,
His dreaming hands wander
   Mid heart's-ease and pansies ;
" 'T is a dream ! 'T is a vision ! "
   Shrieks Mammon aghast ;
" The day's broad derision
   Will chase it at last ;
Ye are mad, ye have taken
A slumbering kraken
   For firm land of the Past ! "
Ah ! if he awaken,
   God shield us all then,
If this dream rudely shaken
   Shall cheat him again !

IX

Since first I heard our North-wind blow,
Since first I saw Atlantic throw
On our grim rocks his thunderous snow,
I loved thee, Freedom ; as a boy
The rattle of thy shield at Marathon
   Did with a Grecian joy
   Through all my pulses run ;
   But I have learned to love thee now
Without the helm upon thy gleaming brow,
   A maiden mild and undefiled
Like her who bore the world's redeeming child ;

And surely never did thine altars glance
With purer fires than now in France;
　While, in their clear white flashes,
　　Wrong's shadow, backward cast,
　Waves cowering o'er the ashes
　　Of the dead, blaspheming Past,
O'er the shapes of fallen giants,
　　His own unburied brood,
Whose dead hands clench defiance
　　At the overpowering Good:
And down the happy future runs a flood
　　Of prophesying light;
It shows an Earth no longer stained with blood,
Blossom and fruit where now we see the bud
　　Of Brotherhood and Right.

ANTI–APIS

Praisest Law, friend? We, too, love it much as they
　　that love it best;
'T is the deep, august foundation, whereon Peace and
　　Justice rest;
On the rock primæval, hidden in the Past its bases be,
Block by block the endeavoring Ages built it up to
　　what we see.

But dig down: the Old unbury; thou shalt find on
　　every stone
That each Age hath carved the symbol of what god to
　　them was known,

Ugly shapes and brutish sometimes, but the fairest
   that they knew;
If their sight were dim and earthward, yet their hope
   and aim were true.

Surely as the unconscious needle feels the far-off load-
   star draw,
So strives every gracious nature to at-one itself with
   law;
And the elder Saints and Sages laid their pious framework right
By a theocratic instinct covered from the people's
   sight.

As their gods were, so their laws were; Thor the
   strong could reave and steal,
So through many a peaceful inlet tore the Norseman's
   eager keel;
But a new law came when Christ came, and not
   blameless, as before,
Can we, paying Him our lip-tithes, give our lives and
   faiths to Thor.

Law is holy : ay, but what law ? Is there nothing more
   divine
Than the patched-up broils of Congress, venal, full of
   meat and wine ?
Is there, say you, nothing higher ? Naught, God save
   us ! that transcends
Laws of cotton texture, wove by vulgar men for
   vulgar ends ?

Did Jehovah ask their counsel, or submit to them a
  plan,
Ere He filled with loves, hopes, longings, this aspiring
  heart of man ?
For their edict does the soul wait, ere it swing round
  to the pole
Of the true, the free, the God-willed, all that makes
  it be a soul ?

Law is holy ; but not your Law, ye who keep the tab-
  lets whole
While ye dash the Law to pieces, shatter it in life and
  soul ;
Bearing up the Ark is lightsome, golden Apis hid
  within,
While we Levites share the offerings, richer by the
  people's sin.

Give to Cæsar what is Cæsar's ? yes, but tell me, if
  you can,
Is this superscription Cæsar's here upon our brother
  man ?
Is not here some other's image, dark and sullied
  though it be,
In this fellow-soul that worships, struggles God-ward
  even as we ?

It was not to such a future that the Mayflower's prow
  was turned,
Not to such a faith the martyrs clung, exulting as
  they burned ;

Not by such laws are men fashioned, earnest, simple,
    valiant, great
In the household virtues whereon rests the unconquer-
    able state.

Ah! there is a higher gospel, overhead the God-roof
    springs,
And each glad, obedient planet like a golden shuttle
    sings
Through the web which Time is weaving in his
    never-resting loom,
Weaving seasons many-colored, bringing prophecy to
    doom.

Think you Truth a farthing rushlight, to be pinched
    out when you will
With your deft official fingers, and your politicians'
    skill?
Is your God a wooden fetish, to be hidden out of
    sight
That His block eyes may not see you do the thing that
    is not right?

But the Destinies think not so; to their judgment-
    chamber lone
Comes no noise of popular clamor, there Fame's
    trumpet is not blown;
Your majorities they reck not; that you grant, but
    then you say
That you differ with them somewhat, — which is
    stronger, you or they?

Patient are they as the insects that build islands in the
    deep;
They hurl not the bolted thunder, but their silent way
    they keep;
Where they have been that we know; where empires
    towered that were not just;
Lo! the skulking wild fox scratches in a little heap of
    dust.

A PARABLE

SAID Christ our Lord, " I will go and see
How the men, my brethren, believe in Me."
He passed not again through the gate of birth,
But made Himself known to the children of earth.

Then said the chief priests, and rulers, and kings,
" Behold, now, the Giver of all good things;
Go to, let us welcome with pomp and state
Him who alone is mighty and great."

With carpets of gold the ground they spread
Wherever the Son of Man should tread,
And in palace-chambers lofty and rare
They lodged Him, and served Him with kingly fare.

Great organs surged through arches dim
Their jubilant floods in praise of Him;
And in church, and palace, and judgment-hall,
He saw His own image high over all.

But still, wherever His steps they led,
The Lord in sorrow bent down His head,
And from under the heavy foundation-stones,
The son of Mary heard bitter groans.

And in church, and palace, and judgment-hall,
He marked great fissures that rent the wall,
And opened wider and yet more wide
As the living foundation heaved and sighed.

"Have ye founded your thrones and altars, then,
On the bodies and souls of living men?
And think ye that building shall endure,
Which shelters the noble and crushes the poor?

"With gates of silver and bars of gold
Ye have fenced My sheep from their Father's fold;
I have heard the dropping of their tears
In heaven these eighteen hundred years."

"O Lord and Master, not ours the guilt,
We build but as our fathers built;
Behold Thine images, how they stand,
Sovereign and sole, through all our land.

"Our task is hard, — with sword and flame
To hold Thine earth forever the same,
And with sharp crooks of steel to keep
Still, as Thou leftest them, Thy sheep."

Then Christ sought out an artisan,
A low-browed, stunted, haggard man,

And a motherless girl, whose fingers thin
Pushed from her faintly want and sin.

These set He in the midst of them,
And as they drew back their garment-hem,
For fear of defilement, " Lo, here," said He,
" The images ye have made of Me ! "

ODE

WRITTEN FOR THE CELEBRATION OF THE INTRODUC-
TION OF THE COCHITUATE WATER INTO THE CITY
OF BOSTON

MY name is Water : I have sped
    Through strange, dark ways, untried before,
By pure desire of friendship led,
    Cochituate's ambassador;
He sends four royal gifts by me :
Long life, health, peace, and purity.

I 'm Ceres' cup-bearer ; I pour,
    For flowers and fruits and all their kin,
Her crystal vintage, from of yore
    Stored in old Earth's selectest bin,
Flora's Falernian ripe, since God
The wine-press of the deluge trod.

In that far isle whence, iron-willed,
    The New World's sires their bark unmoored,

The fairies' acorn-cups I filled
   Upon the toadstool's silver board,
And, 'neath Herne's oak, for Shakespeare's sight,
Strewed moss and grass with diamonds bright.

No fairies in the Mayflower came,
   And, lightsome as I sparkle here,
For Mother Bay State, busy dame,
   I 've toiled and drudged this many a year,
Throbbed in her engines' iron veins,
Twirled myriad spindles for her gains.

I, too, can weave : the warp I set
   Through which the sun his shuttle throws,
And, bright as Noah saw it, yet
   For you the arching rainbow glows,
A sight in Paradise denied
To unfallen Adam and his bride.

When Winter held me in his grip,
   You seized and sent me o'er the wave,
Ungrateful ! in a prison-ship ;
   But I forgive, not long a slave,
For, soon as summer south-winds blew,
Homeward I fled, disguised as dew.

For countless services I 'm fit,
   Of use, of pleasure, and of gain,
But lightly from all bonds I flit,
   Nor lose my mirth, nor feel a stain ;
From mill and wash-tub I escape,
And take in heaven my proper shape.

So, free myself, to-day, elate
  I come from far o'er hill and mead,
And here, Cochituate's envoy, wait
  To be your blithesome Ganymede,
And brim your cups with nectar true
That never will make slaves of you.

LINES

SUGGESTED BY THE GRAVES OF TWO ENGLISH SOLDIERS
ON CONCORD BATTLE-GROUND

THE same good blood that now refills
The dotard Orient's shrunken veins,
The same whose vigor westward thrills,
Bursting Nevada's silver chains,
Poured here upon the April grass,
Freckled with red the herbage new;
On reeled the battle's trampling mass,
Back to the ash the bluebird flew.

Poured here in vain; — that sturdy blood
Was meant to make the earth more green,
But in a higher, gentler mood
Than broke this April noon serene;
Two graves are here: to mark the place,
At head and foot, an unhewn stone,
O'er which the herald lichens trace
The blazon of Oblivion.

These men were brave enough, and true
To the hired soldier's bull-dog creed;

What brought them here they never knew,
They fought as suits the English breed:
They came three thousand miles, and died,
To keep the Past upon its throne;
Unheard, beyond the ocean tide,
Their English mother made her moan.

The turf that covers them no thrill
Sends up to fire the heart and brain;
No stronger purpose nerves the will,
No hope renews its youth again:
From farm to farm the Concord glides,
And trails my fancy with its flow;
O'erhead the balanced hen-hawk slides,
Twinned in the river's heaven below.

But go, whose Bay State bosom stirs,
Proud of thy birth and neighbor's right,
Where sleep the heroic villagers
Borne red and stiff from Concord fight;
Thought Reuben, snatching down his gun,
Or Seth, as ebbed the life away,
What earthquake rifts would shoot and run
World-wide from that short April fray?

What then? With heart and hand they wrought,
According to their village light;
'T was for the Future that they fought,
Their rustic faith in what was right.
Upon earth's tragic stage they burst
Unsummoned, in the humble sock;
Theirs the fifth act; the curtain first
Rose long ago on Charles's block.

TO ———

Their graves have voices; if they threw
Dice charged with fates beyond their ken,
Yet to their instincts they were true,
And had the genius to be men.
Fine privilege of Freedom's host,
Of humblest soldiers for the Right! —
Age after age ye hold your post,
Your graves send courage forth, and might.

TO ———

We, too, have autumns, when our leaves
   Drop loosely through the dampened air,
When all our good seems bound in sheaves,
   And we stand reaped and bare.

Our seasons have no fixed returns,
   Without our will they come and go;
At noon our sudden summer burns,
   Ere sunset all is snow.

But each day brings less summer cheer,
   Crimps more our ineffectual spring,
And something earlier every year
   Our singing birds take wing.

As less the olden glow abides,
   And less the chillier heart aspires,
With driftwood beached in past spring-tides
   We light our sullen fires.

I

By the pinched rushlight's starving beam
　　We cower and strain our wasted sight,
To stitch youth's shroud up, seam by seam,
　　In the long arctic night.

It was not so — we once were young —
　　When Spring, to womanly Summer turning,
Her dew-drops on each grass-blade strung,
　　In the red sunrise burning.

We trusted then, aspired, believed
　　That earth could be remade to-morrow;
Ah, why be ever undeceived?
　　Why give up faith for sorrow?

O thou, whose days are yet all spring,
　　Faith, blighted once, is past retrieving;
Experience is a dumb, dead thing;
　　The victory's in believing.

FREEDOM

ARE we, then, wholly fallen? Can it be
That thou, North-wind, that from thy mountains
　　　　bringest
Their spirit to our plains, and thou, blue sea,
Who on our rocks thy wreaths of freedom flingest,
As on an altar, — can it be that ye
Have wasted inspiration on dead ears,
Dulled with the too familiar clank of chains?
The people's heart is like a harp for years

Hung where some petrifying torrent rains
Its slow-incrusting spray : the stiffened chords
Faint and more faint make answer to the tears
That drip upon them : idle are all words :
Only a golden plectrum wakes the tone
Deep buried 'neath that ever-thickening stone.

We are not free : doth Freedom, then, consist
In musing with our faces toward the Past,
While petty cares and crawling interests twist
Their spider-threads about us, which at last
Grow strong as iron chains, to cramp and bind
In formal narrowness heart, soul, and mind ?
Freedom is re-created year by year,
In hearts wide open on the God-ward side,
In souls calm-cadenced as the whirling sphere,
In minds that sway the future like a tide.
No broadest creeds can hold her, and no codes ;
She chooses men for her august abodes,
Building them fair and fronting to the dawn ;
Yet, when we seek her, we but find a few
Light footprints, leading morn-ward through the dew :
Before the day had risen, she was gone.

And we must follow : swiftly runs she on,
And, if our steps should slacken in despair,
Half turns her face, half smiles through golden hair,
Forever yielding, never wholly won :
That is not love which pauses in the race
Two close-linked names on fleeting sand to trace ;
Freedom gained yesterday is no more ours ;
Men gather but dry seeds of last year's flowers ;

Still there's a charm ungranted, still a grace,
Still rosy Hope, the free, the unattained,
Makes us Possession's languid hand let fall;
'T is but a fragment of ourselves is gained,
The Future brings us more, but never all.

And, as the finder of some unknown realm,
Mounting a summit whence he thinks to see
On either side of him the imprisoning sea,
Beholds, above the clouds that overwhelm
The valley-land, peak after snowy peak
Stretch out of sight, each like a silver helm
Beneath its plume of smoke, sublime and bleak,
And what he thought an island finds to be
A continent to him first oped, — so we
Can from our height of Freedom look along
A boundless future, ours if we be strong;
Or if we shrink, better remount our ships
And, fleeing God's express design, trace back
The hero-freighted Mayflower's prophet-track
To Europe entering her blood-red eclipse.

BIBLIOLATRES

Bowing thyself in dust before a Book,
And thinking the great God is thine alone,
O rash iconoclast, thou wilt not brook
What gods the heathen carves in wood and stone,
As if the Shepherd who from outer cold
Leads all His shivering lambs to one sure fold
Were careful for the fashion of His crook.

There is no broken reed so poor and base,
No rush, the bending tilt of swamp-fly blue,
But He therewith the ravening wolf can chase,
And guide His flock to springs and pastures new;
Through ways unlooked for, and through many
      lands,
Far from the rich folds built with human hands,
The gracious footprints of His love I trace.

And what art thou, own brother of the clod,
That from His hand the crook would'st snatch away
And shake instead thy dry and sapless rod,
To scare the sheep out of the wholesome day?
Yea, what art thou, blind, unconverted Jew,
That with thy idol-volume's covers two
Would'st make a jail to coop the living God?

Thou hear'st not well the mountain organ-tones
By prophet ears from Hor and Sinai caught,
Thinking the cisterns of those Hebrew brains
Drew dry the springs of the All-knower's thought;
Nor shall thy lips be touched with living fire,
Who blow'st old altar-coals with sole desire
To weld anew the spirit's broken chains.

God is not dumb, that He should speak no more;
If thou hast wanderings in the wilderness
And find'st not Sinai, 't is thy soul is poor;
There towers the Mountain of the Voice no less,
Which whoso seeks shall find, but he who bends,
Intent on manna still and mortal ends,
Sees it not, neither hears its thundered lore.

Slowly the Bible of the race is writ,
And not on paper leaves nor leaves of stone ;
Each age, each kindred, adds a verse to it,
Texts of despair or hope, of joy or moan.
While swings the sea, while mists the mountains
      shroud,
While thunder's surges burst on cliffs of cloud,
Still at the prophets' feet the nations sit.

BEAVER BROOK

HUSHED with broad sunlight lies the hill,
And, minuting the long day's loss,
The cedar's shadow, slow and still,
Creeps o'er its dial of gray moss.

Warm noon brims full the valley's cup,
The aspen's leaves are scarce astir ;
Only the little mill sends up
Its busy, never-ceasing burr.

Climbing the loose-piled wall that hems
The road along the mill-pond's brink,
From 'neath the arching barberry-stems,
My footstep scares the shy chewink.

Beneath a bony buttonwood
The mill's red door lets forth the din ;
The whitened miller, dust-imbued,
Flits past the square of dark within.

Beaver Brook

No mountain torrent's strength is here;
Sweet Beaver, child of forest still,
Heaps its small pitcher to the ear,
And gently waits the miller's will.

Swift slips Undine along the race
Unheard, and then, with flashing bound,
Floods the dull wheel with light and grace,
And, laughing, hunts the loath drudge round.

The miller dreams not at what cost
The quivering millstones hum and whirl,
Nor how for every turn are tost
Armfuls of diamond and of pearl.

But Summer cleared my happier eyes
With drops of some celestial juice,
To see how Beauty underlies,
Forevermore each form of use.

And more; methought I saw that flood,
Which now so dull and darkling steals,
Thick, here and there, with human blood,
To turn the world's laborious wheels.

No more than doth the miller there,
Shut in our several cells, do we
Know with what waste of beauty rare
Moves every day's machinery.

Surely the wiser time shall come
When this fine overplus of might,

No longer sullen, slow, and dumb,
Shall leap to music and to light.

In that new childhood of the Earth
Life of itself shall dance and play,
Fresh blood in Time's shrunk veins make mirth,
And labor meet delight halfway.

MEMORIAL VERSES

KOSSUTH

A RACE of nobles may die out,
A royal line may leave no heir;
Wise Nature sets no guards about
Her pewter plate and wooden ware.

But they fail not, the kinglier breed,
Who starry diadems attain;
To dungeon, axe, and stake succeed
Heirs of the old heroic strain.

The zeal of Nature never cools,
Nor is she thwarted of her ends;
When gapped and dulled her cheaper tools,
Then she a saint and prophet spends.

Land of the Magyars! though it be
The tyrant may relink his chain,
Already thine the victory,
As the just Future measures gain.

Thou hast succeeded, thou hast won
The deathly travail's amplest worth;
A nation's duty thou hast done,
Giving a hero to our earth.

And he, let come what will of woe,
Hath saved the land he strove to save;
No Cossack hordes, no traitor's blow,
Can quench the voice shall haunt his grave.

"I Kossuth am : O Future, thou
　　That clear'st the just and blott'st the vile,
O'er this small dust in reverence bow,
　　Remembering what I was erewhile.

"I was the chosen trump wherethrough
　　Our God sent forth awakening breath ;
Came chains? Came death? The strain He blew
　　Sounds on, outliving chains and death."

TO LAMARTINE

1848

I DID not praise thee when the crowd,
　　　'Witched with the moment's inspiration,
Vexed thy still ether with hosannas loud,
　　　And stamped their dusty adoration ;
　　I but looked upward with the rest,
And, when they shouted Greatest, whispered Best.

They raised thee not, but rose to thee,
　　　Their fickle wreaths about thee flinging ;
So on some marble Phœbus the swol'n sea
　　　Might leave his worthless seaweed clinging,
　　But pious hands, with reverent care,
Make the pure limbs once more sublimely bare.

Now thou 'rt thy plain, grand self again,
　　　Thou art secure from panegyric,

Thou who gav'st politics an epic strain,
　　And actedst Freedom's noblest lyric;
　This side the Blessed Isles, no tree
Grows green enough to make a wreath for thee.

Nor can blame cling to thee; the snow
　　From swinish footprints takes no staining,
But, leaving the gross soils of earth below,
　　Its spirit mounts, the skies regaining,
　And unresentful falls again,
To beautify the world with dews and rain.

The highest duty to mere man vouchsafed
　　Was laid on thee, — out of wild chaos,
When the roused popular ocean foamed and chafed,
　　And vulture War from his Imaus
　Snuffed blood, to summon homely Peace
And show that only order is release.

To carve thy fullest thought, what though
　　Time was not granted? Aye in history,
Like that Dawn's face which baffled Angelo
　　Left shapeless, grander for its mystery,
　Thy great Design shall stand, and day
Flood its blind front from Orients far away.

Who says thy day is o'er? Control,
　　My heart, that bitter first emotion;
While men shall reverence the steadfast soul,
　　The heart in silent self-devotion
　Breaking, the mild, heroic mien,
Thou 'lt need no prop of marble, Lamartine.

If France reject thee, 't is not thine,
        But her own, exile that she utters;
Ideal France, the deathless, the divine,
        Will be where thy white pennon flutters,
    As once the nobler Athens went
With Aristides into banishment.

No fitting metewand hath To-day
        For measuring spirits of thy stature;
Only the Future can reach up to lay
        The laurel on that lofty nature,
    Bard, who with some diviner art
Hast touched the bard's true lyre, a nation's heart.

Swept by thy hand, the gladdened chords,
        Crashed now in discords fierce by others,
Gave forth one note beyond all skill of words,
        And chimed together, We are brothers.
    O poem unsurpassed! it ran
All round the world, unlocking man to man.

France is too poor to pay alone
        The service of that ample spirit;
Paltry seem low dictatorship and throne,
        Weighed with thy self-renouncing merit;
    They had to thee been rust and loss;
Thy aim was higher, — thou hast climbed a Cross!

TO JOHN G. PALFREY

THERE are who triumph in a losing cause,
Who can put on defeat, as 't were a wreath
Unwithering in the adverse popular breath,
 Safe from the blasting demagogue's applause;
 'T is they who stand for Freedom and God's laws.

And so stands Palfrey now, as Marvell stood,
Loyal to Truth dethroned, nor could be wooed
 To trust the playful tiger's velvet paws:
And if the second Charles brought in decay
 Of ancient virtue, if it well might wring
Souls that had broadened 'neath a nobler day,
 To see a losel, marketable king
Fearfully watering with his realm's best blood
 Cromwell's quenched bolts, that erst had cracked
  and flamed,
Scaring, through all their depths of courtier mud,
 Europe's crowned bloodsuckers, — how more
  ashamed
Ought we to be, who see Corruption's flood
 Still rise o'er last year's mark, to mine away
 Our brazen idol's feet of treacherous clay!

O utter degradation! Freedom turned
 Slavery's vile bawd, to cozen and betray
 To the old lecher's clutch a maiden prey,
If so a loathsome pander's fee be earned!

And we are silent, — we who daily tread
A soil sublime, at least, with heroes' graves! —
Beckon no more, shades of the noble dead!
Be dumb, ye heaven-touched lips of winds and waves!
Or hope to rouse some Coptic dullard, hid
Ages ago, wrapt stiffly, fold on fold,
With cerements close, to wither in the cold,
Forever hushed, and sunless pyramid!

Beauty and Truth, and all that these contain,
Drop not like ripened fruit about our feet;
We climb to them through years of sweat and pain;
Without long struggle, none did c'er attain
The downward look from Quiet's blissful seat :
Though present loss may be the hero's part,
Yet none can rob him of the victor heart
Whereby the broad-realmed future is subdued,
And Wrong, which now insults from triumph's
car,
Sending her vulture hope to raven far,
Is made unwilling tributary of Good.

O Mother State, how quenched thy Sinai fires!
Is there none left of thy stanch Mayflower breed?
No spark among the ashes of thy sires,
Of Virtue's altar-flame the kindling seed?
Are these thy great men, these that cringe and creep,
And writhe through slimy ways to place and
power? —
How long, O Lord, before Thy wrath shall reap
Our frail-stemmed summer prosperings in their
flower?

Oh for one hour of that undaunted stock
That went with Vane and Sidney to the block!

Oh for a whiff of Naseby, that would sweep,
    With its stern Puritan besom, all this chaff
    From the Lord's threshing-floor! Yet more than
        half
The victory is attained, when one or two,
    Through the fool's laughter and the traitor's
        scorn,
    Beside thy sepulchre can bide the morn,
Crucified Truth, when thou shalt rise anew.

TO W. L. GARRISON

"Some time afterward, it was reported to me by the city offi-
cers that they had ferreted out the paper and its editor; that his
office was an obscure hole, his only visible auxiliary a negro boy,
and his supporters a few very insignificant persons of all colors."
— *Letter of H. G. Otis.*

IN a small chamber, friendless and unseen,
    Toiled o'er his types one poor, unlearned young
        man;
The place was dark, unfurnitured, and mean;
    Yet there the freedom of a race began.

Help came but slowly; surely no man yet
    Put lever to the heavy world with less:
What need of help? He knew how types were set,
    He had a dauntless spirit, and a press.

  I

Such earnest natures are the fiery pith,
    The compact nucleus, round which systems
        grow ;
Mass after mass becomes inspired therewith,
    And whirls impregnate with the central glow.

O Truth ! O Freedom ! how are ye still born
    In the rude stable, in the manger nurst !
What humble hands unbar those gates of morn
    Through which the splendors of the New Day burst !

What ! shall one monk, scarce known beyond his
        cell,
    Front Rome's far-reaching bolts, and scorn her
        frown ?
Brave Luther answered YES; that thunder's swell
    Rocked Europe, and discharmed the triple crown.

Whatever can be known of earth we know,
    Sneered Europe's wise men, in their snail-shells
        curled ;
No ! said one man in Genoa, and that No
    Out of the darkness summoned this New World.

Who is it will not dare himself to trust ?
    Who is it hath not strength to stand alone ?
Who is it thwarts and bilks the inward MUST ?
    He and his works, like sand, from earth are
        blown.

Men of a thousand shifts and wiles, look here !
    See one straightforward conscience put in pawn

To win a world ; see the obedient sphere
    By bravery's simple gravitation drawn !

Shall we not heed the lesson taught of old,
    And by the Present's lips repeated still,
In our own single manhood to be bold,
    Fortressed in conscience and impregnable will ?

We stride the river daily at its spring,
    Nor, in our childish thoughtlessness, foresee,
What myriad vassal streams shall tribute bring,
    How like an equal it shall greet the sea.

O small beginnings, ye are great and strong,
    Based on a faithful heart and weariless brain !
Ye build the future fair, ye conquer wrong,
    Ye earn the crown, and wear it not in vain.

ON THE DEATH OF C. T. TORREY

Woe worth the hour when it is crime
    To plead the poor dumb bondman's cause,
When all that makes the heart sublime,
The glorious throbs that conquer time,
    Are traitors to our cruel laws !

He strove among God's suffering poor
    One gleam of brotherhood to send ;
The dungeon oped its hungry door
To give the truth one martyr more,
    Then shut, — and here behold the end !

O Mother State! when this was done,
  No pitying throe thy bosom gave;
Silent thou saw'st the death-shroud spun,
And now thou givest to thy son
  The stranger's charity, — a grave.

Must it be thus forever? No!
  The hand of God sows not in vain,
Long sleeps the darkling seed below,
The seasons come, and change, and go,
  And all the fields are deep with grain.

Although our brother lie asleep,
  Man's heart still struggles, still aspires;
His grave shall quiver yet, while deep
Through the brave Bay State's pulses leap
  Her ancient energies and fires.

When hours like this the senses' gush
  Have stilled, and left the spirit room,
It hears amid the eternal hush
The swooping pinions' dreadful rush,
  That bring the vengeance and the doom; —

Not man's brute vengeance, such as rends
  What rivets man to man apart, —
God doth not so bring round His ends,
But waits the ripened time, and sends
  His mercy to the oppressor's heart.

ELEGY ON THE DEATH OF DOCTOR CHANNING

I DO not come to weep above thy pall,
    And mourn the dying-out of noble powers;
The poet's clearer eye should see, in all
    Earth's seeming woe, seed of immortal flowers.

Truth needs no champions : in the infinite deep
    Of everlasting Soul her strength abides,
From Nature's heart her mighty pulses leap,
    Through Nature's veins her strength, undying,
        tides.

Peace is more strong than war, and gentleness,
    Where force were vain, makes conquest o'er the
        wave ;
And love lives on and hath a power to bless,
    When they who loved are hidden in the grave.

The sculptured marble brags of death-strewn fields,
    And Glory's epitaph is writ in blood;
But Alexander now to Plato yields,
    Clarkson will stand where Wellington hath stood.

I watch the circle of the eternal years,
    And read forever in the storied page
One lengthened roll of blood, and wrong, and tears,
    One onward step of Truth from age to age.

The poor are crushed; the tyrants link their chain;
  The poet sings through narrow dungeon-grates;
Man's hope lies quenched; and, lo! with steadfast
    gain
  Freedom doth forge her mail of adverse fates.

Men slay the prophets; fagot, rack, and cross
  Make up the groaning record of the past;
But Evil's triumphs are her endless loss,
  And sovereign Beauty wins the soul at last.

No power can die that ever wrought for Truth;
  Thereby a law of Nature it became,
And lives unwithered in its blithesome youth,
  When he who called it forth is but a name.

Therefore I cannot think thee wholly gone;
  The better part of thee is with us still;
Thy soul its hampering clay aside hath thrown,
  And only freer wrestles with the Ill.

Thou livest in the life of all good things;
  What words thou spak'st for Freedom shall not
    die;
Thou sleepest not, for now thy Love hath wings
  To soar where hence thy Hope could hardly fly.

And often, from that other world, on this
  Some gleams from great souls gone before may
    shine,
To shed on struggling hearts a clearer bliss,
  And clothe the Right with lustre more divine.

Thou art not idle : in thy higher sphere
  Thy spirit bends itself to loving tasks,
And strength to perfect what it dreamed of here
  Is all the crown and glory that it asks.

For sure, in Heaven's wide chambers, there is
      room
  For love and pity, and for helpful deeds ;
Else were our summons thither but a doom
  To life more vain than this in clayey weeds.

From off the starry mountain-peak of song,
  Thy spirit shows me, in the coming time,
An earth unwithered by the foot of wrong,
  A race revering its own soul sublime.

What wars, what martyrdoms, what crimes, may
      come,
  Thou knowest not, nor I ; but God will lead
The prodigal soul from want and sorrow home,
  And Eden ope her gates to Adam's seed.

Farewell ! good man, good angel now ! this hand
  Soon, like thine own, shall lose its cunning too ;
Soon shall this soul, like thine, bewildered stand,
  Then leap to thread the free, unfathomed blue :

When that day comes, oh, may this hand grow
      cold,
  Busy, like thine, for Freedom and the Right ;
Oh, may this soul, like thine, be ever bold
  To face dark Slavery's encroaching blight !

This laurel-leaf I cast upon thy bier;
　Let worthier hands than these thy wreath intwine;
Upon thy hearse I shed no useless tear, —
　For us weep rather thou in calm divine!

TO THE MEMORY OF HOOD

ANOTHER star 'neath Time's horizon dropped,
　To gleam o'er unknown lands and seas;
Another heart that beat for freedom stopped, —
　What mournful words are these!

O Love Divine, that claspest our tired earth,
　And lullest it upon thy heart,
Thou knowest how much a gentle soul is worth
　To teach men what thou art!

His was a spirit that to all thy poor
　Was kind as slumber after pain:
Why ope so soon thy heaven-deep Quiet's door
　And call him home again?

Freedom needs all her poets: it is they
　Who give her aspirations wings,
And to the wiser law of music sway
　Her wild imaginings.

Yet thou hast called him, nor art thou unkind,
　O Love Divine, for 't is thy will
That gracious natures leave their love behind
　To work for Mercy still.

Let laurelled marbles weigh on other tombs,
   Let anthems peal for other dead,
Rustling the bannered depth of minster-glooms
   With their exulting spread.

His epitaph shall mock the short-lived stone,
   No lichen shall its lines efface,
He needs these few and simple lines alone
   To mark his resting-place : —

" Here lies a Poet. Stranger, if to thee
   His claim to memory be obscure,
If thou wouldst learn how truly great was he,
   Go, ask it of the poor."

THE VISION OF SIR LAUNFAL

THE VISION OF SIR LAUNFAL

ACCORDING to the mythology of the Romancers, the San Greal, or Holy Grail, was the cup out of which Jesus partook of the Last Supper with His disciples. It was brought into England by Joseph of Arimathea, and remained there, an object of pilgrimage and adoration, for many years in the keeping of his lineal descendants. It was incumbent upon those who had charge of it to be chaste in thought, word, and deed ; but one of the keepers having broken this condition, the Holy Grail disappeared. From that time it was a favorite enterprise of the knights of Arthur's court to go in search of it. Sir Galahad was at last successful in finding it, as may be read in the seventeenth book of the Romance of King Arthur. Tennyson has made Sir Galahad the subject of one of the most exquisite of his poems.

The plot (if I may give that name to anything so slight) of the following poem is my own, and, to serve its purposes, I have enlarged the circle of competition in search of the miraculous cup in such a manner as to include, not only other persons than the heroes of the Round Table, but also a period of time subsequent to the supposed date of King Arthur's reign.

PRELUDE TO PART FIRST

OVER his keys the musing organist,
  Beginning doubtfully and far away,
First lets his fingers wander as they list,
  And builds a bridge from Dreamland for his lay :
Then, as the touch of his loved instrument
  Gives hope and fervor, nearer draws his theme,
First guessed by faint auroral flushes sent
  Along the wavering vista of his dream.

Not only around our infancy
Doth heaven with all its splendors lie ;
Daily, with souls that cringe and plot,
We Sinais climb and know it not.

Over our manhood bend the skies ;
    Against our fallen and traitor lives
The great winds utter prophecies ;
    With our faint hearts the mountain strives ;
Its arms outstretched, the druid wood
    Waits with its benedicite ;
And to our age's drowsy blood
    Still shouts the inspiring sea.

Earth gets its price for what Earth gives us ;
    The beggar is taxed for a corner to die in,
The priest hath his fee who comes and shrives
        us,
    We bargain for the graves we lie in ;
At the devil's booth are all things sold,
Each ounce of dross costs its ounce of gold ;
    For a cap and bells our lives we pay,
Bubbles we buy with a whole soul's tasking :
    'T is heaven alone that is given away,
'T is only God may be had for the asking ;
No price is set on the lavish summer ;
June may be had by the poorest comer.

And what is so rare as a day in June ?
    Then, if ever, come perfect days ;
Then Heaven tries Earth if it be in tune,
    And over it softly her warm ear lays ;

Whether we look, or whether we listen,
We hear life murmur, or see it glisten;
Every clod feels a stir of might,
  An instinct within it that reaches and towers,
And, groping blindly above it for light,
    Climbs to a soul in grass and flowers;
The flush of life may well be seen
    Thrilling back over hills and valleys;
The cowslip startles in meadows green,
    The buttercup catches the sun in its chalice,
And there's never a leaf nor a blade too mean
    To be some happy creature's palace;
The little bird sits at his door in the sun,
    Atilt like a blossom among the leaves,
And lets his illumined being o'errun
    With the deluge of summer it receives;
His mate feels the eggs beneath her wings,
And the heart in her dumb breast flutters and
        sings;
He sings to the wide world, and she to her nest,
In the nice ear of Nature which song is the best?

Now is the high-tide of the year,
    And whatever of life hath ebbed away
Comes flooding back with a ripply cheer,
    Into every bare inlet and creek and bay;
Now the heart is so full that a drop overfills it,
We are happy now because God wills it;
No matter how barren the past may have been,
'T is cnough for us now that the leaves are green;
We sit in the warm shade and feel right well
How the sap creeps up and the blossoms swell;

We may shut our eyes, but we cannot help knowing
That skies are clear and grass is growing;
The breeze comes whispering in our ear,
That dandelions are blossoming near,
    That maize has sprouted, that streams are flowing,
That the river is bluer than the sky,
That the robin is plastering his house hard by;
And if the breeze kept the good news back,
For other couriers we should not lack;
    We could guess it all by yon heifer's lowing, —
And hark! how clear bold chanticleer,
Warmed with the new wine of the year,
    Tells all in his lusty crowing!

Joy comes, grief goes, we know not how;
Everything is happy now,
    Everything is upward striving;
'T is as easy now for the heart to be true
As for grass to be green or skies to be blue, —
    'T is the natural way of living:
Who knows whither the clouds have fled?
    In the unscarred heaven they leave no wake;
And the eyes forget the tears they have shed,
    The heart forgets its sorrow and ache;
The soul partakes the season's youth,
    And the sulphurous rifts of passion and woe
Lie deep 'neath a silence pure and smooth,
    Like burnt-out craters healed with snow.
What wonder if Sir Launfal now
Remembered the keeping of his vow?

Into his soul the vision flew

PART FIRST

I

" My golden spurs now bring to me,
 And bring to me my richest mail,
For to-morrow I go over land and sea
 In search of the Holy Grail;
Shall never a bed for me be spread,
Nor shall a pillow be under my head,
Till I begin my vow to keep;
Here on the rushes will I sleep,
And perchance there may come a vision true
Ere day create the world anew."
 Slowly Sir Launfal's eyes grew dim,
 Slumber fell like a cloud on him,
And into his soul the vision flew.

II

The crows flapped over by twos and threes,
In the pool drowsed the cattle up to their knees,
 The little birds sang as if it were
 The one day of summer in all the year,
And the very leaves seemed to sing on the trees:
The castle alone in the landscape lay
Like an outpost of winter, dull and gray:
'T was the proudest hall in the North Countree,
And never its gates might opened be,
Save to lord or lady of high degree;
Summer besieged it on every side,
But the churlish stone her assaults defied;

I

She could not scale the chilly wall,
Though around it for leagues her pavilions tall
Stretched left and right,
Over the hills and out of sight;
　　Green and broad was every tent,
　　And out of each a murmur went
Till the breeze fell off at night.

III

The drawbridge dropped with a surly clang,
And through the dark arch a charger sprang,
Bearing Sir Launfal, the maiden knight,
In his gilded mail, that flamed so bright
It seemed the dark castle had gathered all
Those shafts the fierce sun had shot over its wall
　　In his siege of three hundred summers long,
And, binding them all in one blazing sheaf,
　　Had cast them forth: so, young and strong,
And lightsome as a locust-leaf,
Sir Launfal flashed forth in his maiden mail,
To seek in all climes for the Holy Grail.

IV

It was morning on hill and stream and tree,
　　And morning in the young knight's heart;
Only the castle moodily
Rebuffed the gifts of the sunshine free,
　　And gloomed by itself apart;
The season brimmed all other things up
Full as the rain fills the pitcher-plant's cup.

V

As Sir Launfal made morn through the darksome gate,
   He was 'ware of a leper, crouched by the same,
Who begged with his hand and moaned as he sate;
   And a loathing over Sir Launfal came;
The sunshine went out of his soul with a thrill,
   The flesh 'neath his armor 'gan shrink and crawl,
And midway its leap his heart stood still
   Like a frozen waterfall;
For this man, so foul and bent of stature,
Rasped harshly against his dainty nature,
And seemed the one blot on the summer morn, —
So he tossed him a piece of gold in scorn.

VI

The leper raised not the gold from the dust:
" Better to me the poor man's crust,
Better the blessing of the poor,
Though I turn me empty from his door;
That is no true alms which the hand can hold;
He gives only the worthless gold
   Who gives from a sense of duty;
But he who gives but a slender mite,
And gives to that which is out of sight,
   That thread of the all-sustaining Beauty
Which runs through all and doth all unite, —
The hand cannot clasp the whole of his alms,
The heart outstretches its eager palms,
For a god goes with it and makes it store
To the soul that was starving in darkness before."

PRELUDE TO PART SECOND

Down swept the chill wind from the mountain
     peak,
  From the snow five thousand summers old;
On open wold and hilltop bleak
  It had gathered all the cold,
And whirled it like sleet on the wanderer's cheek;
It carried a shiver everywhere
From the unleafed boughs and pastures bare;
The little brook heard it and built a roof
'Neath which he could house him, winter-proof;
All night by the white stars' frosty gleams
He groined his arches and matched his beams;
Slender and clear were his crystal spars
As the lashes of light that trim the stars:
He sculptured every summer delight
In his halls and chambers out of sight;
Sometimes his tinkling waters slipt
Down through a frost-leaved forest-crypt,
Long, sparkling aisles of steel-stemmed trees
Bending to counterfeit a breeze;
Sometimes the roof no fretwork knew
But silvery mosses that downward grew;
Sometimes it was carved in sharp relief
With quaint arabesques of ice-fern leaf;
Sometimes it was simply smooth and clear
For the gladness of Heaven to shine through, and
     here
He had caught the nodding bulrush-tops
And hung them thickly with diamond drops,

That crystalled the beams of moon and sun,
And made a star of every one :
No mortal builder's most rare device
Could match this winter-palace of ice ;
'T was as if every image that mirrored lay
In his depth serene through the summer day,
Each fleeting shadow of earth and sky,
   Lest the happy model should be lost,
Had been mimicked in fairy masonry
   By the elfin builders of the frost.

Within the hall are song and laughter,
   The cheeks of Christmas glow red and jolly,
And sprouting is every corbel and rafter
   With lightsome green of ivy and holly ;
Through the deep gulf of the chimney wide
Wallows the Yule-log's roaring tide ;
The broad flame pennons droop and flap
   And belly and tug as a flag in the wind ;
Like a locust shrills the imprisoned sap,
   Hunted to death in its galleries blind ;
And swift little troops of silent sparks,
   Now pausing, now scattering away as in fear,
Go threading the soot-forest's tangled darks
   Like herds of startled deer.

But the wind without was eager and sharp,
Of Sir Launfal's gray hair it makes a harp,
    And rattles and wrings
    The icy strings,
  Singing, in dreary monotone,
  A Christmas carol of its own,

Whose burden still, as he might guess,
Was " Shelterless, shelterless, shelterless ! "
The voice of the seneschal flared like a torch
As he shouted the wanderer away from the porch,
And he sat in the gateway and saw all night
The great hall-fire, so cheery and bold,
Through the window-slits of the castle old,
Build out its piers of ruddy light
Against the drift of the cold.

PART SECOND

I

THERE was never a leaf on bush or tree,
The bare boughs rattled shudderingly ;
The river was dumb and could not speak,
For the weaver Winter its shroud had spun ;
A single crow on the tree-top bleak
From his shining feathers shed off the cold sun ;
Again it was morning, but shrunk and cold,
As if her veins were sapless and old,
And she rose up decrepitly
For a last dim look at earth and sea.

II

Sir Launfal turned from his own hard gate,
For another heir in his earldom sate ;
An old, bent man, worn out and frail,
He came back from seeking the Holy Grail ;

Little he recked of his earldom's loss,
No more on his surcoat was blazoned the cross,
But deep in his soul the sign he wore,
The badge of the suffering and the poor.

III

Sir Launfal's raiment thin and spare
Was idle mail 'gainst the barbed air,
For it was just at the Christmas time;
So he mused, as he sat, of a sunnier clime,
And sought for a shelter from cold and snow
In the light and warmth of long-ago;
He sees the snake-like caravan crawl
O'er the edge of the desert, black and small,
Then nearer and nearer, till, one by one,
He can count the camels in the sun,
As over the red-hot sands they pass
To where, in its slender necklace of grass,
The little spring laughed and leapt in the shade,
And with its own self like an infant played,
And waved its signal of palms.

IV

" For Christ's sweet sake, I beg an alms; "
The happy camels may reach the spring,
But Sir Launfal sees only the grewsome thing,
The leper, lank as the rain-blanched bone,
That cowers beside him, a thing as lone
And white as the ice-isles of Northern seas
In the desolate horror of his disease.

V

And Sir Launfal said, " I behold in thee
An image of Him who died on the tree ;
Thou also hast had thy crown of thorns,
Thou also hast had the world's buffets and scorns,
And to thy life were not denied
The wounds in the hands and feet and side :
Mild Mary's Son, acknowledge me ;
Behold, through him, I give to Thee ! "

VI

Then the soul of the leper stood up in his eyes
   And looked at Sir Launfal, and straightway he
Remembered in what a haughtier guise
   He had flung an alms to leprosie,
When he girt his young life up in gilded mail
And set forth in search of the Holy Grail.
The heart within him was ashes and dust ;
He parted in twain his single crust,
He broke the ice on the streamlet's brink,
And gave the leper to eat and drink,
'T was a mouldy crust of coarse brown bread,
   'T was water out of a wooden bowl, —
Yet with fine wheaten bread was the leper fed,
   And 't was red wine he drank with his thirsty
   soul.

VII

As Sir Launfal mused with a downcast face,
A light shone round about the place ;
The leper no longer crouched at his side,
But stood before him glorified,

Shining and tall and fair and straight
As the pillar that stood by the Beautiful Gate, —
Himself the Gate whereby men can
Enter the temple of God in Man.

VIII

His words were shed softer than leaves from the pine,
And they fell on Sir Launfal as snows on the brine,
That mingle their softness and quiet in one
With the shaggy unrest they float down upon;
And the voice that was softer than silence said,
" Lo, it is I, be not afraid!
In many climes, without avail,
Thou hast spent thy life for the Holy Grail;
Behold, it is here, — this cup which thou
Didst fill at the streamlet for Me but now;
This crust is My body broken for thee,
This water His blood that died on the tree;
The Holy Supper is kept, indeed,
In whatso we share with another's need;
Not what we give, but what we share,
For the gift without the giver is bare;
Who gives himself with his alms feeds three,
Himself, his hungering neighbor, and Me."

IX

Sir Launfal awoke as from a swound:
" The Grail in my castle here is found!
Hang my idle armor up on the wall,
Let it be the spider's banquet-hall;
He must be fenced with stronger mail
Who would seek and find the Holy Grail."

X

The castle gate stands open now,
    And the wanderer is welcome to the hall
As the hangbird is to the elm-tree bough;
    No longer scowl the turrets tall,
The Summer's long siege at last is o'er;
When the first poor outcast went in at the door,
She entered with him in disguise,
And mastered the fortress by surprise;
There is no spot she loves so well on ground,
She lingers and smiles there the whole year round;
The meanest serf on Sir Launfal's land
Has hall and bower at his command;
And there's no poor man in the North Countree
But is lord of the earldom as much as he.

LETTER FROM BOSTON

LETTER FROM BOSTON

December, 1846.

DEAR M——— [1]

     By way of saving time,
I 'll do this letter up in rhyme,
Whose slim stream through four pages flows
Ere one is packed with tight-screwed prose,
Threading the tube of an epistle,
Smooth as a child's breath through a whistle.

     The great attraction now of all
Is the " Bazaar " at Faneuil Hall,
Where swarm the anti-slavery folks
As thick, dear Miller, as your jokes.
There 's GARRISON, his features very
Benign for an incendiary,
Beaming forth sunshine through his glasses
On the surrounding lads and lasses
(No bee could blither be, or brisker), —
A Pickwick somehow turned John Ziska,
His bump of firmness swelling up
Like a rye cupcake from its cup.
And there, too, was his English tea-set,
Which in his ear a kind of flea set,
His Uncle Samuel for its beauty
Demanding sixty dollars duty
('T was natural Sam should serve his trunk ill,
For G., you know, has cut his uncle),

[1] Mr. James Miller McKim.

Whereas, had he but once made tea in 't,
His uncle's ear had had the flea in 't,
There being not a cent of duty
On any pot that ever drew tea.[1]

There was MARIA CHAPMAN, too,
With her swift eyes of clear steel-blue,
The coiled-up mainspring of the Fair,
Originating everywhere
The expansive force without a sound
That whirls a hundred wheels around,
Herself meanwhile as calm and still
As the bare crown of Prospect Hill;
A noble woman, brave and apt,
Cumæan sibyl not more rapt,
Who might, with those fair tresses shorn,
The Maid of Orleans' casque have worn,
Herself the Joan of our Ark,
For every shaft a shining mark.

And there, too, was ELIZA FOLLEN,
Who scatters fruit-creating pollen
Where'er a blossom she can find
Hardy enough for Truth's north wind,

[1] When Mr. Garrison visited Edinburgh in 1846, a handsome silver tea-set was presented to him by his friends in that city. On the arrival of this gift at the Boston custom-house, it was charged with an enormous entrance duty, which would have been remitted if the articles had ever been used. It was supposed that if the owner had not been the leader of the unpopular Abolitionists, this heavy impost would not have been laid on a friendly British tribute to an eminent American.

Each several point of all her face
Tremblingly bright with the inward grace,
As if all motion gave it light
Like phosphorescent seas at night.

There jokes our EDMUND,[1] plainly son
Of him who bearded Jefferson,
A non-resistant by conviction,
But with a bump in contradiction,
So that whene'er it gets a chance
His pen delights to play the lance,
And — you may doubt it, or believe it —
Full at the head of Joshua Leavitt
The very calumet he'd launch,
And scourge him with the olive branch.
A master with the foils of wit,
'T is natural he should love a hit;
A gentleman, withal, and scholar,
Only base things excite his choler.
And then his satire's keen and thin
As the lithe blade of Saladin.
Good letters are a gift apart,
And his are gems of Flemish art,
True offspring of the fireside Muse,
Not a rag-gathering of news
Like a new hopfield which is all poles,
But of one blood with Horace Walpole's.

There, with one hand behind his back,
Stands PHILLIPS buttoned in a sack,

[1] Edmund Quincy.

Our Attic orator, our Chatham;
Old fogies, when he lightens at 'em,
Shrivel like leaves; to him 't is granted
Always to say the word that's wanted,
So that he seems but speaking clearer
The tiptop thought of every hearer;
Each flash his brooding heart lets fall,
Fires what's combustible in all,
And sends the applauses bursting in
Like an exploded magazine.
His eloquence no frothy show,
The gutter's street-polluted flow,
No Mississippi's yellow flood
Whose shoalness can't be seen for mud; —
So simply clear, serenely deep,
So silent-strong its graceful sweep,
None measures its unrippling force
Who has not striven to stem its course;
How fare their barques who think to play
With smooth Niagara's mane of spray,
Let Austin's total shipwreck say.[1]
He never spoke a word too much —
Except of Story, or some such,
Whom, though condemned by ethics strict,
The heart refuses to convict.

[1] On the occasion of the murder of Rev. Elijah P. Lovejoy, editor of an anti-slavery newspaper at Alton, Illinois, an indignation meeting was held in Boston, at which Mr. Austin, Attorney-General of Massachusetts, made a violent proslavery speech, which called forth a crushing reply from Wendell Phillips, who thenceforth became a main pillar of abolitionism.

Beyond, a crater in each eye,
Sways brown, broad-shouldered PILLSBURY,
Who tears up words like trees by the roots,
A Theseus in stout cow-hide boots,
The wager of eternal war
Against that loathsome Minotaur
To whom we sacrifice each year
The best blood of our Athens here
(Dear M., pray brush up your Lemprière).
A terrible denouncer he,
Old Sinai burns unquenchably
Upon his lips ; he well might be a
Hot-blazing soul from fierce Judea,
Habakkuk, Ezra, or Hosea.
His words are red-hot iron searers,
And nightmare-like he mounts his hearers,
Spurring them like avenging Fate, or
As Waterton his alligator.

Hard by, as calm as summer even,
Smiles the reviled and pelted STEPHEN,[1]
The unappeasable Boanerges
To all the Churches and the Clergies,
The grim *savant* who, to complete
His own peculiar cabinet,
Contrived to label 'mong his kicks
One from the followers of Hicks ;
Who studied mineralogy
Not with soft book upon the knee,
But learned the properties of stones
By contact sharp of flesh and bones,

[1] Stephen S. Foster.

I

And made the *experimentum crucis*
With his own body's vital juices;
A man with caoutchouc endurance,
A perfect gem for life insurance,
A kind of maddened John the Baptist,
To whom the harshest word comes aptest,
Who, struck by stone or brick ill-starred,
Hurls back an epithet as hard,
Which, deadlier than stone or brick,
Has a propensity to stick.
His oratory is like the scream
Of the iron-horse's frenzied steam
Which warns the world to leave wide space
For the black engine's swerveless race.
Ye men with neckcloths white, I warn you —
Habet a whole haymow *in cornu.*

A Judith, there, turned Quakeress,
Sits ABBY in her modest dress,[1]
Serving a table quietly,
As if that mild and downcast eye
Flashed never, with its scorn intense,
More than Medea's eloquence.
So the same force which shakes its dread
Far-blazing locks o'er Ætna's head,
Along the wires in silence fares
And messages of commerce bears.
No nobler gift of heart and brain,
No life more white from spot or stain,
Was e'er on Freedom's altar laid
Than hers, the simple Quaker maid.

[1] Abby Kelley.

These last three (leaving in the lurch
Some other themes) assault the Church,
Who therefore writes them in her lists
As Satan's limbs and atheists;
For each sect has one argument
Whereby the rest to Hell are sent,
Which serves them like the Graiæ's tooth,
Passed round in turn from mouth to mouth; —
If any *ism* should arise,
They look on it with constable's eyes,
Tie round its neck a heavy *athe-*,
And give it kittens' hydropathy.
This trick with other (useful very) tricks
Is laid to the Babylonian *meretrix*,
But 't was in vogue before her day
Wherever priesthoods had their way,
And Buddha's Popes with this struck dumb
The followers of Fi and Fum.

Well, if the world, with prudent fear
Pay God a seventh of the year,
And as a Farmer, who would pack
All his religion in one stack,
For this world works six days in seven
And idles on the seventh for Heaven,
Expecting, for his Sunday's sowing,
In the next world to go a-mowing
The crop of all his meeting-going; —
If the poor Church, by power enticed,
Finds none so infidel as Christ,
Quite backward reads his Gospel meek
(As 't were in Hebrew writ, not Greek),

Fencing the gallows and the sword
With conscripts drafted from his word,
And makes one gate of Heaven so wide
That the rich orthodox might ride
Through on their camels, while the poor
Squirm through the scant, unyielding door,
Which, of the Gospel's straitest size,
Is narrower than bead-needles' eyes,
What wonder World and Church should call
The true faith atheistical ?

Yet, after all, 'twixt you and me,
Dear Miller, I could never see
That Sin's and Error's ugly smirch
Stained the walls only of the Church ;
There are good priests, and men who take
Freedom's torn cloak for lucre's sake ;
I can't believe the Church so strong,
As some men do, for Right or Wrong.
But, for this subject (long and vext)
I must refer you to my next,
As also for a list exact
Of goods with which the Hall was packed.

END OF VOLUME I

The Riverside Press

Electrotyped and printed by H. O. Houghton & Co.
Cambridge, Mass, U. S. A.